CORPVS MONVMENTORVM RELIGIONIS DEI MENIS (CMRDM)

I

THE MONUMENTS AND INSCRIPTIONS

ÉTUDES PRÉLIMINAIRES AUX RELIGIONS ORIENTALES DANS L'EMPIRE ROMAIN

PUBLIÉES PAR

M. J. VERMASEREN

TOME DIX-NEUVIÈME

E. LANE

CORPVS MONVMENTORVM RELIGIONIS DEI MENIS
(CMRDM)

I

THE MONUMENTS AND INSCRIPTIONS

LEIDEN
E. J. BRILL
1971

E. LANE

CORPVS MONVMENTORVM RELIGIONIS DEI MENIS
(CMRDM)

I

THE MONUMENTS AND INSCRIPTIONS

WITH 105 PLATES, 36 FIGURES AND 2 FOLDING MAPS

LEIDEN
E. J. BRILL
1971

Copyright 1971 by E. J. Brill, Leiden, Netherlands

All rights reserved. No part of this book may be reproduced or translated in any form, by print, photoprint, microfilm, microfiche or any other means without written permission from the publisher

PRINTED IN THE NETHERLANDS

Dis Manibus
Caroli Bradford Welles

CONTENTS

Preface IX

Catalogue

Graecia 1
Dacia 13
Italia 15
Asia Minor 19
Dubia 156

Addenda 163

Topographical Index 170
Museum Index 172

Plates I–CV and 2 Folding maps . . . . . at the end of the book

PREFACE

I first became interested in the cult of the moon-god Men somewhat more than ten years ago while pursuing graduate studies at Yale University. Prof. C. Bradford Welles encouraged me to write my dissertation on this subject (no comprehensive treatment having appeared since Drexler's article in Roscher's *Lexikon*), and a Fulbright grant to Greece in 1960-61 enabled me to travel to some of the places where Men had been worshipped in antiquity. After the completion of my dissertation, Prof. Harald Ingholt encouraged me to publish my findings in a series of articles in the journal which he edited, *Berytus*. Adverse circumstances under which I was working at the time were largely responsible for the work in the articles, particularly in the first one, not being as thorough as I would have desired. Therefore I was doubly pleased and honored when Prof. Martin Vermaseren offered me the opportunity to present the material to better advantage in the series which he edits. Finally, the Research Council of the University of Missouri generously made available funds for me to travel in Greece and Turkey in 1969 in order to prepare this book.

The present volume is the first of three projected volumes which, like the *Berytus* articles, will include the epigraphical material, the numismatic material, and the testimonia and conclusions, in that order. In this volume I try in general to follow the model of D. Tudor's *Corpus Monumentorum Religionis Equitum Danuviorum*, I (volume 13 of this series). I start with a brief notice of the monument, when and where it was found, where it is now, and its dimensions. Then I list the bibliography, and finally give a detailed description of the monument. Certain deviations, however, are imposed by the material itself. First, unlike Tudor's material, most of the monuments of Men cult are accompanied by inscriptions, which are sometimes quite long. Thus the "description" of the monument will be seen frequently to be almost exclusively composed of the text of the inscription which it bears. Secondly, unlike Tudor's monuments, most of which have found their way into museums, most of the monuments of Men cult (except the coins, which will be treated in a a separate volume) have simply been left *in situ* by their discoverers. Even those which have been transported to museums have in many cases, so far as one can determine, been lost subsequently. This applies especially to those taken to the Evangelike Schole in Smyrna. To retrace the steps of all the travellers in order to find out information as to the present condition and location of all these monuments, would require time and resources far out of all proportion to the results to be gained thereby. I therefore request the reader to bear in mind that many of these monuments about which no recent information is available are either still where they were first discovered, or in the course of war, fire, or demolition have subsequently vanished, without our being able to tell which items belong to which category.

The bibliography endeavors to be reasonably complete, and I hope that I have not omitted from it any significant discussions of the items catalogued. When a reference is made only in passing, however, it is a little hard to determine whether it is significant enough to warrant mentioning; in particular this remark applies to general discussions, and I have consequently made no attempt to include references to the article on Men in Pauly-Wissowa, *Real-Encyclopädie der Klassischen Altertumswissenschaft*.

I have arranged the bibliography in chronological order, except in the cases of certain serial works (e.g. Roscher's *Lexikon*). In these cases I list the reference under the year the serial started, whenever the particular portion referred to may have been written.

The large number of items catalogued and the extensive nature of the bibliography on them would have rendered it too cumbersome, in my opinion, to try to preface to the catalogue, as Tudor does, a complete bibliography of works referred to. Instead, I have given full information concerning each bibliographical item the first time it is mentioned, and afterwards generally refer to it as *op. cit.*, or by abbreviated title. In the case of books, where possible I give the initial of the author's first name (this is harder with authors of journal articles), and the place and date of publication. However, the following standard abbreviations of the titles of journals and corpora are used throughout:

ABSA = Annual of the British School at Athens
AJA = American Journal of Archaeology
AM = Deutsches Archäologisches Institut, Athenische Abteilung, Mitteilungen.
Annuario = Annuario della Scuola Archeologica Italiana di Athene
AS = Anatolian Studies
AZ = Archäologische Zeitung
BCH = Bulletin de Correspondance Hellénique
Belleten = Türk Tarih Kurumu, Belleten
CIG = Corpus Inscriptionum Graecarum
CIL = Corpus Inscriptionum Latinarum
CRAI = Comptes Rendus de l'Académie des Inscriptions et Belles Lettres
HSCP = Harvard Studies in Classical Philology
IG = Inscriptiones Graecae
JHS = Journal of Hellenic Studies
JRS = Journal of Roman Studies
MAMA = Monumenta Asiae Minoris Antiqua
RA = Revue Archéologique
REA = Revue des Études Anciennes
REG = Revue des Études Grecques
RHR = Revue de l'Histoire des Religions
RM = Rheinisches Museum für Philologie
SEG = Supplementum Epigraphicum Graecum
TAM = Tituli Asiae Minoris

The geographical sequence, starting with Attica, has been dictated by the rather paradoxical fact that the oldest preserved monuments of this "oriental" divinity are from that area of Greece.

In epigraphical method I depart somewhat from the Leiden system. That system forces one to make assumptions about the stonecutters' intentions. In the case of the uneducated Greek in which most of the inscriptions here dealt with are composed, such assumptions are difficult to make. I thus use ( ) for any omitted letters which need to be supplied to make the sense evident, without worrying whether we are dealing with deliberate abbreviation or simple mistake; and I use a dot under a letter to indicate that the letter does not appear to be what it should be in order to make sense, without worrying whether this is a mason's mistake or the effect of wear. I do not use the symbol ⟨ ⟩ at all.

I am indebted to many persons and organizations for their cooperation in sharing information with me. In addition to those mentioned at the beginning, let me mention particularly Prof. Theodore V. Buttrey of the University of Michigan; Mr. Cornelius Vermeule of the Museum of Fine Arts, Boston; Mr. Thomas Drew-Bear of Harvard University; the staff of the British Museum; Barbara Levick of St. Hilda's College, Oxford; Mr. J. M. R. Cormack of the University of Aberdeen; the staff of the National Museum, Athens, especially Mrs. Peppa-Delmouzou; the staff of the Agora Excavations, Athens; Angelike Andreiomenou, of the Greek Antiquities Service; the staff oft he museums of Smyrna, Manisa, Afyon, and especially Konya and Yalvaç, all in Turkey; Mr. Dikran Serrafian of Beirut; and the staff of the Musée du Bardo in Tunisia. Final thanks go to Mr. T. A. Edridge of E. J. Brill, for making possible the financing of the illustrations; and to Mrs. Carolyn Jessop, our departmental secretary in Columbia, for her untiring services as typist.

Columbia, Missouri   E. N. LANE

CATALOGUE

GRAECIA

Athenae: Athens, Greece

1. A fragment of a relief of marble, broken all around, found in 1894 in the German excavations between the Areopagus and the Pnyx, south of the Athenian Agora. [1]

Dimensions: Height 17 cm., width 15 cm., thickness 2 cm.

> Bibliography: C. Daremberg and E. Saglio, *Dictionnaire des Antiquités*, Paris 1877-1918, III, ii, 1393. W. Drexler, article in W. H. Roscher, *Lexikon der griechischen und römischen Mythologie*, Leipzig, 1884-1937, col. 2731. H. B. Walters, *Classical Review*, VIII, 1894, p. 229. P. Perdrizet, *BCH*, XX, 1896, p. 81 and Plate XIV. Lane, *Berytus*, XV, 1964, p. 7, no. 2. (hereafter Lane I)

Men is seated on a ram which walks to the right, with a crescent moon behind him. The head of the god, as well as that of the ram, is missing. The god holds a patera in his right hand, stretching it out to two small figures, a man and a woman, worshipping him. A table with offerings (what, exactly, is hard to make out) is to be seen under Men's feet. A small rooster is visible under the table.

2. A relief sculptured on both faces, broken on the left (from the point of view of the side which showed Men). Known since at least 1893. For sale in New York in 1968. Now returned to Münzen und Medaillen, Basel.

Dimensions: Height 45 cm., width 44.5 cm.

> Bibliography: Daremberg-Saglio, *Dictionnaire des Antiquités*, III, p. 1393, fig. 4664; *Katalog der Archaologischen Ausstellung*,[2] Vienna, 1893, no. 1538; P. Perdrizet, *BCH*, XX, 1896, p. 82 and Pl. XV; S. Reinach, *Repertoire des reliefs grecs et romains*, Paris 1909-12, II, p. 150, no. 3; *G. Bakalakis, *Hellenika Amphiglypha* (1946), p. 67 (who dates it ca. 340 B.C.); Lane, I, p. 7, no. 3; Sale Catalogue, *Art of the Ancients*, Andre Emmerich Gallery, N.Y., 1968, no. 44.

[1] If no indication of an object's present location is given, it is to be assumed that it is either still *in situ* or lost.

[2] An asterisk (*) indicates a book I have been unable to consult.

The preserved portion of one side shows the foreparts of a ram facing right with a crescent moon, on which Men must have sat (only part of his drapery is visible); in front of the ram there is a table covered with flat and pyramidal cakes (or fruit?), under which a rooster left faces a hen on the right. Farther to the right, there are four worshippers, two older, bearded men, one young beardless man, and a child, all holding out their right hands in adoration. The opposite side shows a solar divinity in a quadriga driving right. The reliefs on both sides are within an aedicula, with representation of antae, architrave, and roof-tiles. There are traces of an inscription on the architrave of the side with the solar divinity: ···EΛ of the side with Men: ··Θ···I···

3. A fragment of a relief of marble (?), known from an engraving done in the year 1700 and from an earlier inaccurate one of 1687, which shows Men and the young man or woman. Exact circumstances of finding and present whereabouts unknown.

Dimensions unknown.

Bibliography: *Gisbert Cuper, *Harpocrates sive explicatio imagunculae argenteae perantiquae*, Utrecht, 1687 facing p. 198; *Signa antiqua e museo Jacobi de Wilde, veterum poetarum carminibus illustrata et per Mariam filiam aere inscripta*, Amsterdam, 1700, p. 41; Bergk, *AZ*, 1847, p. 47; E. Gerhard, *AZ*, 1850, p. 158-9 and Pl. 15, no. 7; Wolters, *Festschrift für Otto Benndorf*, Vienna, 1898, p. 126; Lane, I, p. 7, no. 4.

No. 3

Men is riding on a ram right, facing forward (no moon appears on the preserved portion of the relief). To the left there is a bearded man kneeling and a younger man or woman behind him. Under the ram there is a table with unclear offerings, to the right there is a woman kneeling, and under the table there are two roosters or rooster and hen.

4. A fragment of a relief broken at top and both sides. There was apparently a lug at the bottom for insertion into a base. Found in the excavations of the Athenian Agora, April 15, 1936, and now in the Agora Museum.

Dimensions: Height 16 cm., width 16.3 cm., thickness 3.7 cm.

Bibliography: Lane, I, p. 7, no. 5 and Pl. II, no. 2.

At the top of the preserved portion we see the lower portion of Men's body, seated slightly left, on a large crescent moon. To the right of the figure, part of his cape hangs down, and in his left hand he holds a staff. Below him, left to right, we see a draped male figure (bare above waist?), with head missing, who holds his right hand clasping an indistinct object up to the god; a low table with a shelf running parallel to the top, a support joining them midway, with two facing roosters, one on either end of the table, and various votive objects (cakes?), conical, round, and oblong; at the extreme right a draped woman likewise holding up an indistinct object to the figure of the god. Before her stand the figures of three children.

5. Three contiguous bricks from a well-head discovered in the Kerameikos ca. 1864. Present whereabouts unknown.

Dimensions unknown.

Bibliography: A. S. Rousopoulos, *Bulletino dell'Instituto di Corrispondenza Archeologica*, 1864, p. 47; C. Lenormant, *Monographie de la Voie Sacrée Éleusinienne*, (1864), I, 85-89 (wild interpretation); idem, article *Eleusinia* in Daremberg-Saglio, note 682; Daremberg-Saglio, III, ii, p. 1397; Perdrizet, *op. cit.*, pp. 78-9; H. Usener, *RM*, LV 1900, p. 295; A. Brueckner, *Der Friedhof am Eridanos*, Berlin 1909, pp. 27-28; *IG*, II², (1913-35), 4876;[1] G. Mylonas, *Eleusis and the Eleusinian Mysteries*, Princeton, 1961, p. 270; Lane, I, p. 8, no. 9.

[1] References to IG II, III (first edition) are not given. The reader can find them from the second edition.

The well-head is without ornamentation, but bears the inscription:

ὁ Πάν, ὁ Μήν, χαίρετε νύμφαι καλαί, ὗε κύε ὑπέρχυε.

Followed by other graffiti, perhaps including a mention of Hekate Enodia.

6. A relief preserved entire. Circumstances of finding unknown (before 1895). Now in the National Museum of Athens.

Dimensions: Height 41 cm., width 43 cm.

> Bibliography: W. Drexler, article in W. H. Roscher, *Lexikon der Griechischen und römischen Mythologie*, Leipzig 1884-1937, col. 2733-4, fig. 10; Y. Smirnoff, article on Men in *Stephanos* (Studies in honor of F. F. Sokolov), St. Petersburg, 1895, pp. 114-117, no. 24, fig. 1; P. Perdrizet, *op. cit.*, pp. 77-8, fig. 5; Svoronos, *Das Athener Nationalmuseum*, Athens 1903-11, Pl. 72, no. 1444; S. Reinach, *Répertoire des Reliefs*, II, p. 356, no. 3; M. P. Nilsson, *Geschichte der Griechischen Religion*, Munich 1950 (2nd ed. 1961), II, Pl. 2, no. 2; Lane, I, p. 8, no. 8 and Plate I, no. 2.

The relief shows, left to right, Pan, naked except for a goatskin cape, clutching an indistinct object to his chest with his right hand, holding a thyrsus in his left; Men, clad in a sleeved and belted chiton with a cape which falls somewhat to his left, and long, tight-fitting pants. The usual Phrygian cap is missing. There is a well-executed crescent at Men's shoulders, and his cape is held in front by a round brooch, perhaps intended for the full moon. In his right hand he holds a long staff, the device on top of which is unclear, and with his left hand he clasps a rooster in front of his chest. To the right is a nymph or votary, heavily draped, holding her right arm in front of her chest, the left down and slightly out. Both arms are wrapped in the drapery. Pan and the female figure both face slightly inwards, Men full front.

7. A stone with relief and inscription, first reported in 1874 from the collection of Saburoff, the Russian ambassador in Athens. Now in the Staatliches Museum, Berlin.

Dimensions: Height 40 cm., length 33.7 cm., thickness 4 cm., height of letters .9 cm.

> Bibliography: Wieseler, *Nachrichten der Gesellschaft der Wissenschaften, Göttingen*, 1874, p. 14; idem, *Abhandlungen Ges. Wiss. Gött*, XIX, 1874, p. 34; Drexler, *op. cit.*, col. 2733; Daremberg-Saglio, III, ii, p. 1397;

No. 7

Beschreibung der Antiken Skulpturen, Königliche Museen, Berlin, 1891, pp. 262-3; Perdrizet, *op. cit.*, p. 80, no. 3; C. Michel, *Recueil d'inscriptions grecques*, Paris 1897-1927, no. 1690; *IG*, II², 4818; Lane, I, p. 9, no. 10; L. Vidman, *Sylloge Inscriptionum Religionis Isiacae et Sarapiacae*, Berlin, 1969, p. 15, no. 27.

The relief consists of a seven-pointed star in a large crescent, all within a square field. Under it there is the following inscription:

Ἱερεὺς στολιστὴς Ἴσιδος
καὶ Σεράπιδος Αὐρ. Ἐπαφρόδει-
τος τῷ Οὐρανίῳ Μηνὶ εὐχα-
[ρ]ιστήριον ἀνέθηκα.

At the end there are traces of other letters, perhaps added later.

Peiraieus: Piraeus, Greece

8. Marble altar, probably found in the excavations of the Metroon in 1855. Now in the Louvre, Paris.

Dimensions: Height 52 cm., width of base 53.5 cm., width of shaft 34 cm., thickness of shaft 36.5 cm., height of letters 2 cm.

Bibliography: *IG*, II², 4687a; A. Dain, *Inscriptions Grecques du Musée du Louvre*, Paris 1933, p. 162, no. 183; L. Robert, *Revue Archéologique*, 1933, II, p. 145; Robert, *BCH*, LX, 1936, pp. 206ff.; Lane, I, p. 8, no. 7.

The stone bears the inscription:

Δημήτριος
καὶ ἡ γυνὴ
'Ερώτιον Μηνὶ
ἐπὶ ἱερέας
Γλαύκου.

Robert dates this inscription to the late 3rd cent. B.C.

9. An inscribed marble statue base, with hole for statue. Found ca. 1879, now in the Epigraphical Museum, Athens.

Dimensions: Height 15 cm., length 75 cm., thickness 66 cm., height of letters 1.5 cm., hole ca. 55 × 35 cm.

> Bibliography: C. Wachsmuth, *Die Stadt Athen im Alterthum*, Leipzig 1874-90, II, i, p. 163, note 1; Daremberg-Saglio, III, ii, p. 1397; *Kumanudes, *Athenaion*, 8, 1879, p. 294, no. 4; P. Foucart, *BCH*, IV, 1880, p. 129; Drexler, *op. cit.* col. 2730; P. Perdrizet, *BCH*, XX, 1896, p. 75, note 1; Michel, *Recueil*, no. 1689; *IG*, II², 4685; Lane, I, p. 8, no. 6.

The stone bears the inscription:

Διονύσιος καὶ Βαβυλία τῷ Μηνὶ τὸ ἱερὸν ἀνέθεσαν.

Thoricus: Thorikos, Greece

10. A relief, broken in two pieces, missing the upper right corner and part of the bottom. Exact circumstances of finding unknown, but known since 1881. Now in the National Museum, Athens.

Dimensions: Height 24 cm., length 32 cm., height of letters 1 cm.

> Bibliography: *L. von Sybel, *Katalog der Skupturen zu Athen*, Marburg 1881, p. 72, no. 390; *A. Milchhöfer, *Die Museen Athens*, Athens 1881, p. 24; Drexler, *op. cit.*, col. 2730-31, fig. 9; Smirnoff, *Stephanos*, p. 122, no. 28, fig. 4; Perdrizet, *op. cit.*, p. 83 and fig. 6; Svoronos, *Das Athener Nationalmuseum*, p. 355, Pl. 69, no. 1406; Reinach, *Répertoire des Reliefs*, II, p. 356, no. 4; *IG*, II², 4684; Nilsson, *GGR*, II, Plate 2, no. 1; Lane, I, p. 6, no. 1 and Plate I, no. 1.

The whole relief is framed like an aedicula with the representation of an architrave surmounted by roof-tiles at the top. Along the architrave we read the inscription:

Μιτραδάτης καὶ ἡ γυνὴ Μηνὶ [ἀνέθηκαν].

Under the architrave we have from left to right: a veiled and draped woman in an attitude of adoration facing right; a draped and bearded man, his right shoulder bare, also facing right in an attitude of adoration; a table bearing four votive cakes (?)—indistinct shape, round, conical, and one with slices clearly marked on its top; on the right, Men, seated facing left on a large rooster which strides out of the building to the right—its head and legs are missing. Men is dressed as usual, but this time also has the Phrygian cap, missing on no. 6. The crescent at his shoulders was probably indicated in paint (as were the reins of the horses on the obverse of no. 2). In his right hand he holds a patera toward the votaries. His left hand was apparently around the bird's neck.

Sunium: Sounion, Greece

11. An inscribed stone. Found ca. 1868.
Dimensions unknown.

> Bibliography: *Kumanudes, *Palingenesia*, Sept. 23, 1868, no. 3; Drexler, *op. cit.*, col. 2732; *IG*, II², 4856; Lane, I, p. 9, no. 12.

The stone bears the inscription:

> Ξά[ν]θος Μ[ηνὶ Τυράννῳ].

See nos. 12 and 13.

12. An inscribed stone, found ca. 1868, "südlich von Ergasteria, im Lauriongebiet" (Drexler). Now in Epigraphical Museum, Athens.

Dimensions: Height 68 cm., width 27 cm., thickness 7 cm., height of letters, lines 1-6, 2.4 cm., rest of inscription .8 cm.

> Bibliography: W. Gurlitt, *Philologus*, XXVII, 1868, pp. 729-35; *A. Cordella, *Le Laurion*, Marseille, 1871, p. 34-36; P. Foucart, *Des Associations Religieuses chez les Grecs*, Paris, 1873, pp. 119-27; Daremberg-Saglio, III, ii, p. 1397; Drexler, *loc. cit.*; Milchhöfer, *AM*, XII, 1887, p. 300, no. 279; Perdrizet, *op. cit.*, p. 84; *IG*, II², 1365; Lane, I, p. 9, no. 13.

At the top of the stone there is a crescent, roughly inscribed, perhaps painted. Then follows this inscription, of which the last four lines are written on the right flank of the stone:

> Ξάνθος
> Λύκιος

καθειδρούσατο
ἱερὸν τοῦ
Μηνὸς
Τυράννου
αἱρετίσαντος τοῦ θε-
οῦ, ἐπ' ἀγαθῇ τύχῃ καὶ μηθένα ἀκάθαρτον προσάγειν. Καθαριζέστω δὲ ἀπὸ σκόρ-
δων καὶ χοιρέων. Καὶ μηθένα
θυσιάζειν ἄνευ τοῦ καθι-
δρουσαμένου. Ἐὰν δέ τις βιάσηται, ἀπρόσδεκτος ἡ θυσία παρὰ
τοῦ θεοῦ. Παρέχειν δὲ τῶι
θεῶι τὸ καθῆκον, δεξιὸν σκέλος καὶ δορὰν καὶ ἔλαιον ἐπὶ βωμὸν καὶ λύχ(ν)ον καὶ σπονδήν. Καὶ
ἀπὸ νεκροῦ καθαρίζεσται δεκα-
τ(αί)αν, ἀπὸ γυναικέων ἑβ(δ)ομαία(ν),
ἀνδροφόνον μηδὲ περὶ τὸν τόπον, ἀπὸ δὲ φθορᾶς τεττερα-
κοσταίαν, ἀπὸ δὲ γυναικὸς λου-
σάμενοι κατακέφαλα αὐθειμε-
ρί. Εὐίλατος γένοιτο ὁ θεὸς τοῖς
θεραπεύουσιν ἁπλῇ τῇ ψυχῇ.
Ἐὰν δέ τινα ἀνθρώπινα πάσχῃ ἢ
ἀσθενήσῃ ἢ ἀποδημήσῃ, θεραπευέ[τω]
τὸν θεὸν ὦι ἂν αὐτὸς παραδοῖ. Ὃς ἂν δ[ὲ]
πολυπραγμονήσῃ ἢ περιεργάσητα[ι],
ἁμαρτίαν ὀφ[ει]λέτω Μηνὶ Τυράννῳ,
ἣν οὐκ ἐξειλάσεται. Διδότω κε-
φαλὴ-
ν καὶ
πόδας (καὶ)
στηθύ-
νιον.

13. An inscribed stone found at the same place and time as the preceding. Now in the Epigraphical Museum, Athens.

Dimensions: Height 89 cm., width 73 cm., thickness 9.5 cm., height of letters .9 cm.

> Bibliography: Gurlitt, *loc. cit.*; Cordella, *loc. cit.*; Foucart, *loc. cit.*; Daremberg-Saglio, *loc. cit.*; Drexler, *loc. cit.*; Milchhöfer, *loc. cit.*; Perdrizet, *loc. cit.*; Michel, *Recueil*, 988; P. Stengel, *Hermes*, XXXVI, 1901, p. 331-2; J. Prott and L. Ziehen, *Leges Graecorum Sacrae e Titulis Collectae*, Leipzig 1906, II, 1, 149, p. 148-153; *IG*, II², 1366; W. Dittenberger, *Sylloge Inscriptionum Graecarum*³, Leipzig, 1915-20, no. 1042; Lane, I, p. 9, no. 14.

At the top of the stone there is a crescent, well incised, which seems to spread out horseshoe fashion at left top. The stone was apparently fixed by lug at bottom.

Under it there is the following inscription: [1]

Ξάνθος Λύκιος Γαίου 'Ορβίου καθειδρύσατο ἱερ[ὸν τοῦ Μηνὸς]
Τυράννου, αἱρετίσαντος τοῦ θεοῦ, ἐπ' ἀγαθῆ τύχη. Καὶ [μηθένα]
ἀκάθαρτον προσάγειν. Καθαριζέστω δὲ ἀπὸ σκόρδων κα[ὶ χοιρέων]
καὶ γυναικός. Λουσαμένους δὲ κατακέφαλα αὐθήμερον εἰσ[πορεύ-]
εσθα(ι). Καὶ ἐκ τῶν γυναικέων διὰ ἑπτὰ ἡμερῶν λουσαμένην κ[ατα-]
κέφαλα εἰσπορεύεσθαι αὐθήμερον. Καὶ ἀπὸ νεκροῦ διὰ ἡμερῶν δ[έκα]
καὶ ἀπὸ φθορᾶς ἡμερῶν τετταράκοντα, καὶ μηθένα θυσιάζειν ἄνε[υ]
τοῦ καθειδρυσαμένου τὸ ἱερόν. Ἐὰν δέ τις βιάσηται, ἀπρόσδεκτος
ἡ θυσία παρὰ τοῦ θεοῦ. Παρέχειν δὲ τῶι θεῶι τὸ καθῆκον, δεξιὸν
σκέλος καὶ δορὰν καὶ κεφαλὴν καὶ πόδας καὶ στηθύνιον καὶ ἔλαιον
ἐπὶ βωμὸν καὶ λύχνον καὶ σχίζας καὶ σπονδήν, καὶ εὐείλατος
γένοιτο ὁ θεὸς τοῖς θεραπεύουσιν ἁπλῆ τῆ ψυχῆ. Ἐὰν δέ τινα
ἀνθρώπινα πάσχη ἢ ἀσθενήση ἢ ἀποδημήση που, μηθένα ἀνθρώπων ἐξουσίαν ἔχειν, ἐὰν μὴ ὦι ἂν αὐτὸς παραδῶι. Ὅς ἂν δὲ πολυ-
πραγμονήση τὰ τοῦ θεοῦ ἢ περιεργάσηται, ἁμαρτίαν ὀφειλέτω Μηνὶ
Τυράννωι, ἣν οὐ μὴ δύναται ἐξειλάσασθαι. Ὁ δὲ θυσιάζων τῆ ἑβδόμη
τὰ καθήκοντα πάντα ποιείτωι τῶι θεῶι. Λαμβανέτωι τῆς θυσίας ἧς
ἂν φέρη σκέλος καὶ ὦμον, τὰ δὲ λοιπὰ κατακοπτέτω (ἐν τῷ) ἱερῶι. Εἰ δέ τις
εἰ δέ τις προσφέρει θυσίαν τῶι θεῶι, ἐγ νουμηνίας μέχρι πεντεκαι-
δεκάτης. Ἐὰν δέ τις τράπεζαν πληρῶι τῶι θεῶι, λαμβανέτω τὸ ἥμισ[υ].
Τοὺς δὲ βουλομένους ἔρανον συνάγειν Μηνὶ Τυράννω, ἐπ'ἀγαθῆι τύ[χηι].

---

[1] The letters in this inscription are badly formed and often resemble other letters than those intended. Rather than trying to indicate this on the text, I refer the reader to the photograph.

Ὁμοίως δὲ παρέξουσιν οἱ ἐρανισταὶ τὰ καθήκοντα τῶι θεῶι, δε[ξιὸν]
σκέλος καὶ δορὰν καὶ κοτύλην ἐλαίου καὶ χοῦν οἴνου καὶ να[στὸν χοινι-]
κιαῖον καὶ ἐφίερα τρία καὶ κολλύβων χοίνικες δύο καὶ ἀκρό[αμα, ἐ-]
ὰν κατακλιθῶσιν οἱ ἐρανισταὶ καὶ στέφανον καὶ λημνίσ[κον].
Καὶ εὐείλατος γένοιτο ὁ θεὸς τοῖς ἁπλῶς προσπορευομένοις.

Eretria: Eretria, Greece

14. A terracotta relief-figurine, found ca. 1959 in a tomb of the 3rd century B.C. Now in local museum.
Dimensions unavailable.

> Bibliography: A. Andreiomenou, *Archaiologikon Deltion*, XVI, 1960, ii, p. 150; Lane, I, p. 10, no. 1.

Men, his head and left arm broken off, sits frontally on a large crescent, which is raised from the surface of a disk, which is broken at top and right, and which forms the background of the representation. Men holds a patera in his outstretched right hand. At his feet, serving as support for the crescent and the disk, is a large spotted animal (panther?).

Thasus: Thasos, Greece

15. An inscribed altar, broken at top. Found in 1886 by J. T. Bent at Aliki on the island of Thasos.
Dimensions: Height 32 cm., width 20 cm.

> Bibliography: Drexler, *op. cit.*, col. 2730; E. L. Hicks, *JHS*, VIII, 1887, p. 411, no. 5; Perdrizet, *op. cit.*, p. 76, note 2; *IG*, XII, viii, (1909), 587; Lane, I, p. 11, no. 2.

The stone bears the following inscription:

> illegible line above
> ἀνέθη-
> κεν θεῷ
> Μηνὶ Τυράν-
> νῳ Διονύσῳ
> Λαέου χάριν [ποι-

οὖ]σα · · ·
illegible line below

(Hicks' restoration).

Rhodus: Rhodes, Greece

16. An inscribed stone found ca. 1892 (?) "ad viam quae Sümbüllü fert" (IG).

Dimensions: Length 1.03 m., height 41 cm., thickness 75 cm., height of letters 1.2 cm.

> Bibliography: Drexler, *op. cit.*, col. 2699; *Selivanov, *Topog. Rod.*, 1892, p. 131; *IG*, XII, i, (1895), 162; Perdrizet, *op. cit.*, p. 76, note 1; Lane, I, p. 11, no. 3.

The stone bears the following inscription, the first part, including the name of the person honored, being lost:

τ[ι]μαθ[έ]ντος ὑπὸ ʿΑλιαστᾶν ʾΑθαναϊαστᾶν ʿΕρμαϊαστᾶν ʾΑ[ρ]ιστιδείων
κοινοῦ χρυσέωι στεφάνωι, καὶ ὑπὸ Διὸς Σωτηριαστᾶν
Σαραπιαστᾶν κοινοῦ θαλλίνωι στεφάνωι,
καὶ ὑπὸ Σαραπιαστᾶν χρυσέωι στεφάνωι · καὶ ὑπὸ Μηνιαστᾶν
ʾΑφροδισιαστᾶν κοινοῦ χρυσέωι στεφάνωι, καὶ ὑπὸ Σωτηριαστᾶν
ʾΑσκλαπιαστᾶν Ποσειδανιαστᾶν ʾΑθαναϊαστᾶν ʾΑφροδισιαστᾶν
ʿΕρμιαστᾶν Ματρὸς θεῶν κοινοῦ χρυσέωι στεφάνωι [κα]ὶ ὑπὸ
ʿΕστιαστᾶν κοινοῦ θαλλίνωι στεφάνωι.

Lindus: Lindos, Greece (island of Rhodes)

17. An oblong altar decorated with 6 bucrania, garlands, ribbons, and little chains (IG) found in 1886 (?) in the village (?) of Lartos, near the garden of Stephen Ganotis (Tiganotis) (so IG).

Dimensions: Height 76 cm., width 78 cm., thickness 44 cm., height of letters 2 cm.

> Bibliography: Drexler, *op. cit.*, col. 2699; E. Loewy, *Archäologisch-Epigraphische Mitteilungen aus Österreich-Ungarn*, X, 1886, p. 219, no. 23; *IG*, XII, i, 917; Perdrizet, *op. cit.*, p. 76, note 1; Lane, I, p. 12, no. 4.

The following inscription is arranged around a crown in a square field:

Τὸ κοινὸν   Διόδοτος
τὸ Μηνιαστᾶν   ἐγγενὴς
ἐτίμασε   υἱὸς
Ἡφαιστίωνα   Ἡφαιστίωνος
Ἀντιοχῇ θαλλίνῳ στεφάνῳ
    Χρηστοὶ χαίρετε.

It is likely that the Hephaistion who is being honored here was a native of Antioch in Pisidia. His son is expressly stated to be a native of Lindos, so the father must have migrated there.

Delus: Delos, Greece

18. A white stone that appears to have been part of a larger monument, found in 1881 in Serapaeon C of the island. In gymnasium in 1911. Now still *in situ*.

Dimensions: Height 25 cm., width 49 cm., height of letters 2.2 cm.

> Bibliography: A. Hauvette-Bernault, *BCH*, VI, 1882, p. 345, no. 65; Drexler, *op. cit.*, col. 2730; Perdrizet, *BCH*, XX, 1896, p. 75, note 2; *P. Roussel, *Les Cultes Égyptiens à Délos du IIe siècle av. J.C.*, Nancy, 1916, no. 63; *IG*, XI, (1927), 1291; Lane, I, p. 12, no. 5; J. Marcadé, *Au Musée de Délos*, Paris, 1969, pp. 399 and 411; L. Vidman, *op. cit.*, p. 67, no. CE 63.

The stone bears the inscription in the upper left corner:

Τάοσα Μηνί.

19. A white stone which appears to have been part of a larger monument, found 1910 in Serapaeum B of the island. Still *in situ*.

Dimensions: Height 15.5 cm., length 40.5 cm., thickness 15 cm., height of letters 1.0 to 1.6 cm.

> Bibliography: *P. Roussel, *op. cit.*, no. 34; *IG*, XI, 1292; Lane, I, p. 12, no. 6; J. Marcadé, *locc. citt.*; L. Vidman, *op. cit.*, p. 63, no. CE 34.

The stone bears the inscription, centered:

Ἀριστοκύδης Μηνί.

DACIA

Sarmezigetusa: Sarmezigetusa Rumania

20. An inscribed altar found in 1911 at Oraştie (Várhely), now in the orphanage of the reformed church in Brios (?).
Dimensions: Height 23 cm., width 19 cm. (?)

> Bibliography: B. Janó, *Archeologiai Ertesitö*, XXXII, 1912, p. 50; *Archäologischer Anzeiger*, 1912, col. 530-1; C. Daicoviciu, *Dacia*, VII-VIII, 1937-40, p. 310; *Année Epigraphique*, 1944, no. 38; Lane, I, p. 12, C and *Berytus*, XVII, 1967, p. 44, no. 5 (hereafter Lane II).

The stone bears the following inscription (Daicoviciu's interpretation):

> Meni
> Cilvastion(o)
> G(aius) Petr(onius) Iustus
> corn(icularius) proc(uratoris)
> ex voto

Potaissa: Turda, Romania

21. An inscribed altar found 1910 at Dealul Cetatii (Varhegy), now in National Antiquities Museum, Bucharest.
Dimensions: Height 70 cm., width 23 cm., max. letter size 3 cm.

> Bibliography: *Archaeologiai Ertesitö*, XXXV, 1915, p. 45, fig. 3; N. Gostar, *Dacia*, N.S., IV, 1960, pp. 519-522; Robert, *REG*, LXXV, 1962, p. 192, no. 245; Lane, I, p. 12, C; *E. Bujor, *Apulum*, VI, 1967, p. 186-9, no. 3 and fig. 1-3; *Année Epigraphique*, 1967, no. 398; *SEG*, XXIV, 1969, no. 1156.

The stone bears the following inscription:

> Μηνὶ 'Άνει-
> ική(τ)ῳ Aur.
> Marcianus

[s]ignifer
l[e]g(ionis) voto
posuit.

Bujor wishes to interpret: l(egionis) G(eminae)

No. 21

ITALIA

Ostia: Ostia, Italy

22. An inscribed stone, exact circumstances of find unknown. Now in Ostia Museum according to *IG*.
Dimensions unavailable.

Bibliography: *IG*, XIV, (1890), 913; Lane, I, p. 13, no. 1.

The stone bears an inscription heavily restored on the basis of Latin parallels:

εξεμ
τονυμιν θ[εοῖσι]
ἀθανάτοις ['Ρείῃ τε καὶ "Αττει]
Μηνοτυ[ράννῳ······]
···ια···

Roma: Rome, Italy

23. An inscribed altar found in the early 17th century in the foundations of St. Peter's basilica.
Dimensions unavailable.

Bibliography: *CIL*, VI, (1876), 499, on the basis of early 17th cent. copies; H. Dessau, *Inscriptiones Latinae Selectae*, Berlin, 1892-1914, 4147; Lane, I, p. 13, no. 2; R. Duthoy, *The Taurobolium*, Leiden, 1969, p. 14, no. 13.

The stone bears the inscription:

Matri Deum Magnae
Idaeae Summae Pa-
renti, Hermae, et Attidi
Menotyranno Invicto
Clodius Hermogianus Caesarius
V(ir) C(onsularis) Procons. Africae
Praefect. Urbis Romae
XVvir S(acris) F(aciundis) taurobolio

>   crioboliooque perfecto XIII Kal. Aug. diis animae
>   suae mentisque costodibus
>   aram dicavit
>   D(omino) N(ostro) Gratiano Aug. ter
>   et ...... Aequitio conss.

The inscription is dated to 374 A.D.

24. An inscribed altar found in the early 17th century in the foundations of St. Peters basilica.
Dimensions unavailable.

> Bibliography: *CIL*, VI, 500, on the basis of copies of the early 17th century; F. Cumont, *Textes et monuments figurés relatifs aux mystères de Mithra*, Brussels, 1899, II, no. 19; Dessau, *ILS*, 4148; M. J. Vermaseren, *Corpus Inscriptionum et Monumentorum Religionis Mithriacae*, Hague, 1956-60, I, p. 204, no. 513; Lane, I, p. 13, no. 3.

The stone bears the following inscription:
M(atri) D(eum) M(agnae) I(daeae)
et Attidi Meno-
tyranno conser-
vatoribus suis Cae-
lius Hilarianus V(ir) C(onsularis)
Duodecimbyr
Urbis Romae
P(ater) S(acrorum) et Hieroceryx
I(nvicti) M(ithrae) S(acerdos) D(ei) L(iberi) S(acerdos) D(eae)
Hecate
D(omino) N(ostro) Gratiano Aug.
et Merobaude Conss. III Idus
Maias.
The inscription is dated to 377 A.D.

25. An inscribed altar found in the early 17th century in the foundations of St. Peter's basilica.
Dimensions unavailable.

> Bibliography: *CIL*, VI, 501 on the basis of early 17th century copies; Dessau, *ILS*, 4149; Lane, I, p. 14, no. 4; Duthoy, *op. cit.*, p. 14, no. 14.

ITALIA

The stone bears the inscription:
>M(atri) D(eum) M(agnae) I(daeae)
>et Attidi Sancto
>Menotyranno
>Q. Claudius Flavianus
>V(ir) C(onsularis) Pont(ifex) Maior
>XV vir S(acris) F(aciundis) Septem-
>vir Epulonum
>Pontifex Dei Solis
>taurobolio criobo-
>lioque percepto
>aram dicavit
>Nonis Aprilibus
>FFLL (*i.e., Flaviis*) Merobaude II
>et Saturnino
>conss.

The inscription is dated 383 A.D.

26. A fragmentary inscribed altar found in the spring of 1949 near S. Lorenzo in Piscibus. Now in Vatican Museum?
Dimensions unavailable.

>Bibliography: B. M. Apollonj-Ghetti, A. Ferrua, E. Josi, and E. Kirschbaum, *Esplorazioni sotto la confessione di San Pietro in Vaticano eseguite negli anni 1940-49*, Vatican City, 1951, pp. 14-15, fig. 2; *Année Epigraphique*, 1953, no. 237; Vermaseren, *op. cit.*, I, p. 165, no. 378; Lane, I, p. 14, no. 5.

(Sextius Rusticus was proconsul of Africa 371-3)
The stone bears the inscription:
>Diis [Magnis]
>M(atri) D(eum) M(agnae) I(daeae) et A[ttidi Meno-]
>tyranno [Sextius Rus-]
>ticus V(ir) C(onsularis) [et inlust-]
>ris Pater Pat[rum Dei In-]
>victi Mithr[ae......]

27. An inscribed reused altar found in October, 1949, under St. Peter's square. Now in Vatican Museum.
Dimensions unavailable.

Bibliography: Apollonj-Ghetti, et al., *loc. cit.*, fig. 3; *Année Epigraphique*, 1953, no. 238; Vermaseren, *op. cit.*, I, p. 205, no. 515; Lane, I, p. 14, no. 6; Duthoy, *op. cit.*, p. 24, no. 34.

The stone bears the following inscription:
        Diis Magnis
        M(atri) D(eum) M(agnae) I(daeae) et
        Attidi Sancto Menotyranno
        Alfenius Ceionus Iulianus
        Kamenius V(ir) C(onsularis) VIIvir Epul(onum)
        Pater et Hieroceryx sacr(orum) S(ummi) I(nvicti)
        Mitrae, Hierofanta Haecatae,
        Archboucolus Dei Liberi
        aram taurobolio criobolio-
        que percepto dicabit
        die XIII Kal. Aug. D(omino) N(ostro) Gratiano
        Aug. III et Equitio Conss.
The date is 374 A.D., the same day as no. 23.

ASIA MINOR

Smyrna: İzmir, Turkey

28. An inscribed stele of marble found ca. 1875 at Sibile Tepe, on the East slope of the Pagos. Now in Athens Epigraphical Museum, no. 4227.

Dimensions: Height 1.30 cm., maximum width 49 cm., maximum thickness 9 cm.

Bibliography: *Mouseion kai Bibliotheke tes Evangelikes Scholes*, II, i, 1876, no. ρξϛ'; Drexler, *op. cit.*, col. 2697; Smirnoff, *op. cit.*, p. 91, no. 5; Dittenberger, *SIG³*, no. 996; Lane I, p. 14, no. 1 and II, p. 44, no. 2.

The stone, broken in nine pieces, bears the following inscription:

Ἀπολλώνιος Μητροδώρου Σπάρος
ὁ πατὴρ τοῦ γενομένου ἱερέως Ἀπο[λ-]
λωνίου τοῦ Ἀπολλωνίου Σπάρου τοῦ
Ἡλίου Ἀπόλλωνος Κισαυλοδδηνοῦ, ἀ-
νέθηκεν τῶι θεῶι καὶ τῆι πόλει τὰ κατασκευ-
ασθέντα ὑπ' αὐτοῦ, λαβὼν κατὰ ψήφισμα τὴν
ἀναγραφὴν ποιήσασθαι αὐτῶν ἐν στήλη. Καί
ἔστιν αὐτὸς ὁ θεὸς ἐπ[ὶ β]ήματος μαρμαρίνου
καὶ ἡ παρακειμένη τῶι θεῶ[ι] τράπεζα λίθου Λεσβί-
ου ἔχουσα πόδας ἀνα[γλύ]πτους γρύπας καὶ πρὸ αὐτῆς ἀβάκηον μαρμάρινον πρὸς τὴν χρῆσιν τῶν
θυσιαζόντων καὶ θυμιατήριον τετράγωνον κα-
τεσκευασμένον πέτρας Τηίας ἔχον περίπυρον
σιδηροῦν καὶ ἄγαλμα μαρμάρινον Ἀρτέμιδος ἐ-
πὶ παραστάδι μυλίνῃ καὶ Μηνὸς ἄγαλμα ἐπὶ βάσει
μαρμαρίνῃ, καὶ τράπεζα ποικίλη τετράγωνος
καὶ βωμὸς μαρμάρινος ἔχων ἀετὸν ἐν ἑαυτῷ
Διὸς καὶ ναὸς ἐξυλωμένος καὶ κεκεραμωμέ-
νος καὶ τεθυρωμένος καὶ κεκλειδωμένος,
ἐν ᾧ καθείδρυται ἀγάλματα Πλούτωνος Ἡ-
λίου καὶ Κούρης Σελήνης ἐπὶ βήματος
ἐμπεφιασμένα ἔχοντα καὶ παστῆον ξύλι-

νον ναοειδὲς καὶ παστὸν λινοῦν, καὶ παρ' ἑκατέ-
ρᾳ τῶν εἰσόδων βωμὸς Φωκαϊκὸς καὶ κλεῖν
κεχρυσωμένην καὶ ἐμπεφιασμένην πρὸς
τὴν λογήαν καὶ πομπὴν τῶν θεῶν καὶ στεγνὰ
ἐπίπεδα καὶ ἐπ' αὐτῶν στοὰν κατῳκοδομημέ-
νην καὶ κεκεραμωμένην πρὸς τὴν οἴκησιν τῶν
ἱεροδούλων καὶ τὸν θεὸν θεραπευόντων καὶ
τὴν ἐνδώμησιν τοῦ τεμένους καὶ θεμελί-
ωσιν ἐν τετραγόνῳ διὰ σπαράγματος, ἵνα
ἦν ἐπίπεδον ἐν ὁμαλῷ τὸ τέμενος, καὶ ὅπλα
τῶι θεῶι παρακείμενα τοῦ κόσμου χάριν
σιδηρᾶ ὀκτώ.

Magnesia ad Maeandrum: Tekke, Turkey

29. A stone of blue marble, rough on underside and backside, smoothed on others. A hole, 12 cm. by 18 cm. by 7 cm. deep, in the top. In 1900 in the house of a Çerkes, in Tekke. Found before 1900 in the area west of the theater.

Dimensions: Height 20 cm., width 32 cm., depth 26 cm., height of letters 2.5 cm., interlineation 2.5 to 4 cm.

> Bibliography: Drexler, *op. cit.*, col. 2697; Kern, *Archäologischer Anzeiger*, 1894, p. 124; *Kern, *Wochenschrift für Klassische Philologie*, 1894, col. 907; Perdrizet, *op. cit.*, p. 70; O. Kern, *Die Inschriften von Magnesia am Mäander*, Berlin, 1900, pp. 143-4, no. 227; Lane, I, p. 14, no. 2.

The stone bears the inscription:

Φίλητος ὁ παρὰ
Χαριδήμου ἀ-
νέθηκεν τῷ Μη-
νί.

Pergamum: Bergama, Turkey

30. An altar with sculptured decoration found in the Hera sanctuary of Pergamum in 1910-11.

Dimensions: Height 1.10 m., width and depth each 49 cm.

Bibliography: A. Ippel, *AM*, XXXVII, 1912, p. 285, no. 10; Lane, I, p. 14, no. 3.

The stone has two goat's heads, one on each side, which are connected with thick garlands; in the middle of each garland there is a grape-cluster on the surrounding band. On the front there is a mask over the garland, on the left side a cista, on the right side a two-handled kantharos, and behind two poppy-heads. Over the mask in the front there is the following inscription:

Μηνὶ Τυράννῳ
Ἰούλιος Ἀσκληπιακός.

Gyölde, Turkey (area of Kula)

31. Marble (?) plaque, found before 1880 in the *parekklesi* of John the Baptist in Gyölde. Taken to the Museum of the *Evangelike Schole* in Smyrna, and apparently subsequently lost.
Dimensions unknown.

Bibliography: *Mouseion kai Bibliotheke*, III, 1-2, 1878-80, p. 167, no. τλζ'; Drexler, *op. cit.*, col. 2700, no. 1; Perdrizet, *op. cit.*, p. 58, no. 4; J. Keil and A. von Premerstein, *Bericht über eine Zweite Reise in Lydien*, Österreichische Akademie der Wissenschaften, Denkschriften, Philosophische-Historische Klasse, LIV, ii, 1911 (hereafter K-P, II Reise), p. 95, col. 2; Lane, I, p. 15, Lydia no. 1.

The stone bears a leg in relief and the inscription:

Μηνὶ Ἀξιεττηνῷ ἐξ Ἐπι-
κράτου Ἑρμογένης ἐπὶ χά-
ριτος εὐχήν.

32. Marble (?) plaque, found at the same time and same place in Gyölde as the above, likewise transported to the museum of the *Evangelike Schole*. Apparently lost.
Dimensions unknown.

Bibliography: *Mouseion kai Bibliotheke*, III, 1-2, 1878-80, p. 167, no. τλθ'; Drexler, *op. cit.*, col. 2700, no. 2; Perdrizet, *op. cit.*, p. 58, no. 3; Lane, I, Lydia, no. 2.

The stone bears two eyes in relief and the inscription:

Μηνὶ Οὐρανίῳ

Μηνὶ Ἀξιοττηνῷ
···λία Ποπλίου

33. Marble (?) plaque found before 1829 in Gyölde in church of Hagios Theodoros.
Dimensions unknown.

> Bibliography: *CIG*, (1828-77), 3448; G. Keppel, *Narrative of a journey across the Balcan, also of a visit to Aizani and the newly discovered ruins in Asia Minor in the years 1829-30*, London, 1831, II, p. 357, no. 1; P. LeBas and W. H. Waddington, *Voyage Archéologique en Grece et en Asie Mineure*, Paris, ca. 1870, III, i, p. 217, no. 680; Drexler, col. 2700, no. 4; Lane, I, p. 15, Lydia, no. 4.

The stone bears a crescent moon in relief and the inscription:

Ἔτους σζ', μη(νὸς) Ξανδικοῦ βι', κατὰ ἐπιταγὴν Μηνὸς Ἀρτεμιδώρου Ἀξιοττηνοῦ, Ἤπιος Τ[ι]βερίου Φιλοκάλου δοῦλος ὑπὲρ ἑαυτοῦ καὶ τῶν τέκνων ἀνέθηκεν.

No indication of line-division is given. 122-123 A.D., Sullan era (as are all dates until number 103)

34. A low base of white marble with mouldings above and below, found before 1870 in the church of Hagios Taxiarches in Gyölde, west wall, outside, left of entrance.
Dimensions: Height 24 cm., width 54 cm., height of letters .8 cm. to 1.4 cm. First three lines of inscription on upper moulding.

> Bibliography: LeBas-Waddington, *op. cit.*, III, i, p. 214-15, no. 678; Drexler, *op. cit.*, col. 2702, no. 12; W. Ramsay, *BCH*, XXII, 1898, p. 239; F. Poland, *Geschichte des griechischen Vereinswesens*, Leipzig, 1909, p. 218; K-P, II Reise, p. 94, no. 183; Lane, I, p. 16, no. 10.

The stone bears the following inscription:

161-2 A.D.

[Ἔτ]ους σμς', ἀνέθηκαν οἱ κα[τ]αλουστικοὶ Μητρ[ὸς 2-3]
[2-3] καὶ Μηνὸς Τιάμου καὶ Μηνὸς Πετραείτου τὸ [ἄγαλ-]
μα τοῦ Διονύσου.
Ἰουλιανός, Δαμᾶς, Εὐσχήμων, Ἄπφιον, Ἀπφῦς, Μᾶρκος, Πόπλιος, Σεκοῦνδος, Πρωτόκτητος, Ἑρμοκράτης,
Μητρόδωρος, Δαμᾶς, Ἀπφίας, Ἑρμογένης, Δαμᾶς, Μη-

νόφιλος, Ἀπολλώνιος, Ἡραΐς, Ἑρμοκράτης, Ἀπολλώνιος, Γλύκων, Ἀπολλώνιος, Ἄμμιον, Τρύφων, Μελτίνη, Ἑρμογένης, Παπίας, Ἑρμογένης, Ἀπφίας, Ἀσκλᾶς, Μελτίνη, Ἑρμογένης, Νεικόμαχος, Πεία, Μᾶρκος, Τύχη, Ἀπελλᾶς, Ἀλέξανδρος, Μελτίνη, Σώστρατος, Νεικίας, Ἰουλιανή, Μητροφάνης, Ἀθηναΐς.

35. A stone with relief and inscription, found ca. 1886, perhaps brought to Gyölde from Aivatlar. Now in Leiden.

Dimensions: Height 98 cm., width at bottom 44.3 cm., width under entablature 36.9 cm., width at entablature 41.8 cm., thickness 4.7 cm.

> Bibliography: *Mouseion kai Bibliotheke*, V, i, 1884-5, p. 54, no. υλγ′; Drexler, *op. cit.*, col. 2703, no. 16; S. Reinach, *RA*, 1886, I, p. 156; G. Leemans, *Grieksche Opschriften uit Klein-Azie*, (Amsterdam Academy, Verhandelingen, Afdeeling Letterkunde, XVII, ii), 1886, pp. 10-11, no. 4 and Plate I, no. 4; H. J. Polak, *Mnemosyne*, XV, 1887, p. 252ff., no. 4; Ramsay, *JHS*, X, 1889, p. 226, no. 20; J. Wright, *HSCP*, VI, 1895, p. 72, note 6; Perdrizet, *op. cit.*, p. 58, no. 2; Steinleitner, *Die Beicht in Zusammenhange mit der sakralen Rechtspflege in der Antike*, Munich and Leipzig, 1913, pp. 22-23, no. 4; H. W. Pleket, *Greek Inscriptions in the Rijksmuseum van Oudheden at Leiden*, 1958 (= Oudheidkundige Mededeelingen, Suppl. to vol. 38), App. II, no. 4 and Pl. XIV; Lane, I, p. 17, no. 14.

The stone bears two breasts, a leg, and two eyes in relief and the following inscription:

Θεᾷ Ἀνάειτι καὶ Μηνὶ Τιάμου
Τύχη καὶ Σωκράτης καὶ Ἀμμιανὸς καὶ Τρόφιμος οἱ Ἀμμίου καὶ Φιλήτη καὶ Σωκρατία
αἱ Ἀμμιάδος ποιήσαντες τὸ ἱεροποίημα εἰλασάμενυ Μητέραν Ἀνάειτιν ὑπὲρ τέκνων καὶ
θρεμμάτων ἔνγραφον ἔστησαν.
Ἔτους τκα′, μη(νὸς) Ξανδικοῦ.

The year is 236-237 A.D.

36. Stone of unknown type, found before 1870, exact circumstances unknown.

Dimensions unknown.

Bibliography: Le Bas-Waddington, III, i, p. 215, no. 685; Drexler, *op. cit.*, col. 2704, no. 21; Lane, I, p. 17, no. 18.

The stone bears an inscription of which little can be made out from the copy:

ρειπαρεν
Μηνεὶ Τυρά[ννῳ]
μουκληρον
· · · μοκαιτα
ιανεθι

37. Fragment of stele of white marble, wider at bottom, broken above and below. Found before 1870 in the *parekklesi* of John the Baptist, Gyölde.
Dimensions: Height 20 cm., width 38 cm., thickness 7.5 cm., height of letters 1.7 cm.
Bibliography: Le Bas-Waddington, *op. cit.*, III, i, p. 215, no. 686; K-P, II Reise, p. 95, no. 184; Lane, I, p. 19, no. 27.

The top of the preserved portion of the stone bears a relief which seems to represent the mule mentioned in the inscription. Underneath the traces of the relief, the following inscription can be read:

['Αξι]ο[τη]ν[ῷ] ἐ[ξ] 'Επικρ[α-]
[το]υ 'Ελπὶς 'Ανδρονίκο[υ]
εὐξαμένη ὑπὲρ τοῦ ἡμι-
όνου εὐχήν.

38. Fragment of a stele of white marble broken on all sides. Found before 1911 in the *parekklesi* of Hagios Theodoros in Gyölde.
Dimensions: Maximum height 11 cm., maximum width 19.5 cm., thickness 4 cm., height of letters 1.2 cm.
Bibliography: K-P, II Reise, p. 95, no. 185; Lane, I, p. 18, no. 22.

The stone bears traces of an inscribed crescent, and the inscription:

Μηνὶ 'Αξιο[ττηνῷ]

39. Pyramidal stele of white marble, found by G. M. A. Hanfmann at Gyölde, now in Sardis Excavation collection.

Dimensions: Height 32 cm., width 31 cm. at bottom, 23.5 cm. at top, thickness 4.2 cm.

> Bibliography: L. Robert, *Nouvelles Inscriptions de Sardes*, Paris, 1964, pp. 35-6 and Plate III, no. 1; Lane, II, p. 46, no. 8.

The stone bears a representation of a woman standing, her right hand uplifted in prayer. Under the relief there is the following inscription:

     Ἔτους τιγ΄, μη(νὸς) Γορπιαίου   228-9 A.D.
     ηι΄. Μηνὶ Μοτελλείτῃ
     Τροφίμη ὑπὲρ Ἰουλιανοῦ
     τοῦ θρεπτοῦ εὐχὴν
     ἀνέστησεν.

Koresa?: Ayazviran, Turkey (area of Kula)

40. Plaque (of marble?), found before 1885 in house of Halil Kechagianni Moustafa.

Dimensions: Height 33 cm., width 24 cm., thickness 4 cm.

> Bibliography: *Mouseion kai Bibliotheke*, 1885/6, 2, p. 804, no. φος΄; Drexler, *op. cit.*, col. 2700, no. 3; Smirnoff, *op. cit.*, p. 93, no. 15; Perdrizet, *op. cit.*, p. 58, top, no. 6; K-P, II Reise, p. 105; P. Herrmann, *Ergebnisse einer Reise in Nordostlydien*, Denkschriften der Österreichischen Akademie der Wissenschaften, Philosophisch-Historische Klasse, LXXX, 1962, p. 45, note 176; Lane, I, p. 15, Lydia no. 3.

The stele bears the following inscription:

     Μηνὶ Ἀξιοττηνῷ Ἀθη-
     νίων ὑπὲρ Ὀνησίμη-
     ς τῆς τεθραμένης
     εὐχήν.

41. Marble plaque with relief and inscription, found before 1898 in Ayazviran.

Dimensions unknown.

> Bibliography: Drexler, *op. cit.*, col. 2702, no. 9; K. Buresch, *Reisebericht II*, Akademie der Wissenschaften, Leipzig, Berichte, Philosophisch-Historische Klasse, XLVI, 1894, p. 95; Perdrizet, *op. cit.*, p. 58,

top, no. 7; Buresch, *Aus Lydien*, Leipzig, 1898, p. 79, no. 39; Lane, I, p. 15, Lydia no. 7.

The stone bears a relief showing a man, a child and a woman, left to right, all praying with uplifted arms. Under the relief there is the following inscription:

[Τα]τιανὸς Γλαῦκος καὶ ᾽Αμμιανὴ φι-
[λ]όθεοι Μηνὶ Μοτυλείτῃ εὐχαριστ-
[ία]αν ἔθοντο εὐχόμενοι ἀεὶ ὑπὲρ
[θ]ρεπτῆς γένει πρώτης Σαβειν-
ῆς [······] ἥνπερ σώσειες σὺ [···]

42. Stele of white marble, wider at bottom, broken at bottom, injured top right and left. Found in 1911 in a field just east of Ayazviran, transported to house of Secbekoğlu Mustafa.

Dimensions: Height 42 cm., width at top 34.5 cm., at bottom 37 cm., thickness 5 cm., height of letter 1.5 to 1.6 cm.

Bibliography: K-P, II Reise, p. 103, no. 204; Steinleitner, *op. cit.*, p. 10, no. 1; M. Rostovzeff, *Social and Economic History of the Roman Empire*², Oxford, 1957, p. 656, note 6; Herrmann, *op. cit.*, p. 45, note 174; Lane, I, p. 18, no. 20.

The stone bears the inscription:

[Με]γάλη Μήτ[ηρ Ταζη-]
νὴ καὶ Μὶς Λαβάνας [καὶ]
Μὶς ᾽Αρτεμιδώρου Δό-
ρου κώμην βασιλεύον-
τες. Ἔτους σκη΄, μη(νὸς) Δαισί-
ου Σε(βαστῇ), ᾽Ιουλία Μητρὰ ἀνέ-
στησε στήλλην ἐπιζητη-
σάντων τῶν θεῶν τὴν γ[ε-]
γόνουσαν ἁμαρτίαν ὑ[πὸ]
················· 143-4 A.D.

43. Stele of marble, decreasing towards top, lug at bottom. Found before 1900, presumably in Ayazviran. Transported to *Evangelike Schole* in Smyrna. Now apparently lost.

Dimensions: Height 1.10 m., width at top 42 cm., at bottom 50 cm. Molding at top broken.

Bibliography: *A. Fontrier, *Harmonia*, 20 and 31 May 1900, no. 2; J. Zingerle, *Österreichisches Archäologisches Institut, Jahreshefte*, XXIII, 1926, Beiblatt, cols. 1-15 and fig. 1; *SEG*, IV, 1930, p. 123, no. 647; O. Eger, *Festschrift P. Koschaker*, 1939, vol. III, p. 290, for these documents in general; Rostovzeff, *SEHRE*[2], p. 656, note 6; Herrmann, *op. cit.*, p. 30, note 102; Lane, I, p. 18, no. 24.

At the top of the stele there is an incised outline crescent. Under it there is the following inscription:

Μεγάλη Μήτηρ Ἀνάειτις Ἄζι-   114-115 A.D.
τα κατέχουσα καὶ Μεὶς Τιάμου
καὶ αἱ δυνάμεις αὐτῶν. Ἑρμογένης καὶ Ἀπολλώνιος οἱ Ἀπολλωνίου Μίδου ἀπὸ Σύρου μανδρῶν
πλαζομένων χοίρων τρειῶν Δημαινέτου καὶ Παπίου ἐξ Ἀζί-
των καὶ προσμισγόντων αὐτῶν
προβάτοις τοῦ Ἑρμογένου καὶ Ἀ-
πολλωνίου, παιδίου αὐτῶν βόσ-
κοντος πενταετοῦς, καὶ ἀπαγα-
γόντων ἔσω, ζητοῦντος οὖν τοῦ
Δημαινέτου καὶ τοῦ Παπίου οὐ-
κ ὡμολόγησαν διά τινα ἀχαριατί-
αν. Ἐπεστάθη οὖν τῆς θεοῦ τὸ σκῆπτρον καὶ τοῦ Κυρίου τοῦ Τιάμου.
Καὶ μὴ ὁμολογησάντων αὐτῶν ἡ
θεὸς οὖν ἔδειξεν τὰς ἰδίας δυνάμις καὶ ἱλάσαντο αὐτὴν τελευ-
τήσαντος τοῦ Ἑρμογένου ἡ γυνὴ
αὐτοῦ καὶ τὸ τέκνον καὶ Ἀπολλώνιος ὁ ἀδελφὸς τοῦ Ἑρμογένου. Καὶ
νῦν αὐτῇ μαρτυροῦμεν καὶ εὐλο-
γοῦμεν μετὰ τῶν τέκνων.
Ἔτους ρϙθ'.

44. Stele of marble, decreasing in size towards top, found before

1900, presumably in Ayazviran, transported to *Evangelike Schole* in Smyrna. Now apparently lost.

Dimensions: Height 1 m., width at top 31 cm., at bottom 45 cm. Moulding at top.

Bibliography: *Fontrier, *Harmonia*, 20 and 31 May, 1900, no. 5; Zingerle, *op. cit.*, col. 16-23 and fig. 2; *SEG*, IV, p. 124, no. 648; Herrmann, *op. cit.*, p. 30, note 102 and p. 60, note 231; Lane, I, p. 18, no. 25.

The stone bears the following inscription:

Ἔτους σμα′, μη(νὸς) Πανήμου β′,   156-157 A.D.
Μεγάλη Ἄρτεμις Ἀνάει-
τις καὶ Μὴν Τιάμου. Ἐπὶ
Ἰουκοῦνδος ἐγένετο ἐν
διαθέσι μανικῇ καὶ ὑπὸ πάντων διεφημίσθη ὡς ὑπὸ
Τατίας τῆς πενθερᾶς αὐ-
τοῦ φάρμακον αὐτῷ δίδοσ-
θαι, ἡ δὲ Τατίας ἐπέστησεν
σκῆπτρον καὶ ἀρὰς ἔθηκεν
ἐν τῷ ναῷ ὡς ἱκανοποιοῦ-
σα περὶ τοῦ πεφημίσθαι αὐ-
τὴ ἐν συνειδήσι τοιαύτῃ.
Οἱ θεοὶ αὐτὴν ἐποίησαν ἐ[ν]
κολάσει, ἣν οὐ διέφυγεν. Ὁ-
μοίως καὶ Σωκράτης, ὁ υἱὸς
αὐτῆς, παράγων τὴν ἴσοδον
τὴν ἐς τὸ ἄλσος ἀπάγουσαν,
δρέπανον κρατῶν ἀμπελοτ[ό-]
μον ἐκ τῆς χειρὸς ἔπεσεν
αὐτῷ ἐπὶ τὸν πόδαν καὶ οὕ-
τως μονημέρῳ κολάσει ἀ-
πηλλάγη. Μεγάλοι οὖν οἱ θεοὶ οἱ ἐν Ἀζίττοις. Ἐπέστησαν
λυθῆναι τὸ σκῆπτρον καὶ τὰς
ἀρὰς τὰς γενομένας ἐν τῷ
ναῷ, ἃς λῦσαν τὰ Ἰουκούνδου
καὶ Μοσχίου, ἔγγονοι δὲ τῆς
Τατίας, Σωκράτεια καὶ Μοσχᾶς

καὶ Ἰουκοῦνδος καὶ Μενεκράτης, κατὰ πάντα ἐξειλασάμενοι
τοὺς θεοὺς καὶ ἀπὸ νοῖν εὐλογοῦ-
μεν στηλλογραφήσαντες τὰς δυνάμις τῶν θεῶν.

45. Stele of marble with pediment, found before 1900, presumably in Ayazviran, then transported to *Evangelike Schole*. Now apparently lost.

Dimensions: Height 70 cm.

    Bibliography: *Fontrier, *loc. cit.*, no. 4; Zingerle, *op. cit.*, col. 27, no. 4; *SEG*, IV, p. 125, no. 650; Lane, I, p. 19, no. 26.

The stone bears the following inscription:

    Θεᾷ Ἀνάειτι καὶ   211-212 A.D.
    Μηνὶ Τιάμου. Σωκρά-
    τεια κ(αὶ) Βασσίλλα
    κ(αὶ) Ἀπολλωνὶς κ(αὶ) Πρό-
    κλος κ(αὶ) Τρόφιμος
    ἀπέδωκαν τὸ ἱ[ε-]
    ροποίημα εὐχαρισ-
    τοῦντες. Ἔτους σϟϛ',
    μη(νὸς) Λώου β'.

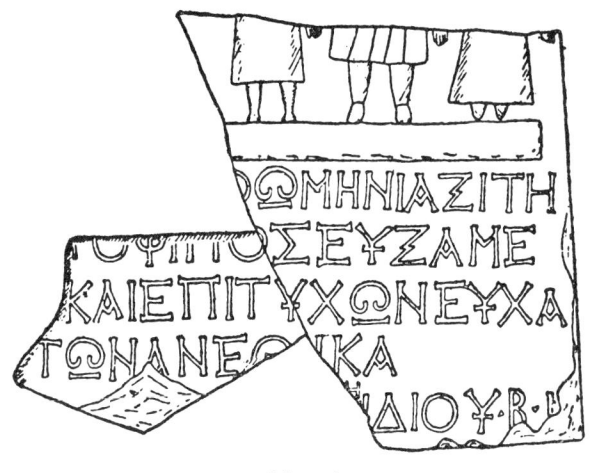

No. 46

46. Two fragments of a stele of bluish marble, preserving part of original right margin. Found in 1911, piece *a* (larger, right) on outside of house of Tartaroğlu Mehmet Çanç in Ayazviran, piece *b* (smaller, left) in house of Kadiroğlu Suleiman.

Dimensions: Height 25 cm., width (two pieces together) 32 cm., thickness 6.3 cm., height of letters 2.2 cm.

  Bibliography: K-P, II Reise, p. 105, no. 205; Herrmann, *op. cit.*, p. 45, note 176; Lane, I, p. 18, no. 21.

The stone bears the remains of three figures in relief—a girl, a man, and a woman (there may have been others)—standing on a projecting ledge, and under them the inscription:

[Θεῷ ἐπηκ]όῳ Μηνὶ Ἀξιτη-
[νῷ Τ]ρόφιμος εὐξάμε-
[νος] καὶ ἐπιτυχὼν εὐχα-
[ρισ]τῶν ἀνέθηκα
[······] μη(νὸς) Δίου βι΄.

47. Stele of white marble, broken in two, moulding at top. Found by P. Herrmann before 1962.

Dimensions: Height 1.04 m., width 42 cm., thickness 8 cm., height of letters 1.5 cm.

  Bibliography: Herrmann, *op. cit.*, p. 24, no. 18, Plate VI, no. 1; Robert, *REG*, LXXVI, 1963, p. 166-7, no. 224; Lane, I, p. 50, no. A1.

The stone bears a relief showing a female figure, a crescent, and a double axe, followed by the inscription:

118-9 A.D.

Ἔτους σγ΄, μη(νὸς) Ἀρτεμεισίου ς΄, ἐ-
πὶ Τροφίμῃ Ἀρτεμιδώρου Κι-
κιννάδος κληθεῖσα ὑπὸ τοῦ
θεοῦ ἰς ὑπηρεσίας χάριν μὴ
βουληθοῦσα ταχέως προσελ-
θεῖν ἐκολάσετο αὐτὴν καὶ μα-
νῆναι ἐποίησεν. Ἠρώτησε οὖν Μητέρα Ταρσηνὴν καὶ Ἀπόλλωνα Τάρσι-
ον καὶ Μῆνα Ἀρτεμιδώρου Ἀξι-
οττηνὸν Κόρεσα κατέχοντα

καὶ ἐκέλευσεν στηλλογραφ-
ηθῆναι νέμεσιν καὶ καταγρά-
ψαι ἐμαυτὸν ἰς ὑπηρεσίαν
τοῖς θεοῖς.

48. Stele (fragmentary) of white marble, broken at top, bottom, and right. Found by P. Herrmann before 1962.

Dimensions: Height 24 cm., width 22 cm., thickness 7.5 cm., height of letters 1.4 cm.

> Bibliography: Herrmann, *op. cit.*, p. 46, no. 40, Plate XIII, no. 1; Lane, I, p. 51, no. A6.

The stone bears slight traces of a relief and the following inscription:

Ἔτους σξβ', μη(νὸς) Ξ[ανδικοῦ···]   177-8 A.D.
Θεῷ Ἀξιοττη[νῷ ··············]
βούλων Τατιο[················]
[··· Ἐ]ρμογένου[·············]

49. Small bomos with hollow on center of top. Top front surface somewhat broken. Located in 1886 in the Turkish sanctuary of Ayazviran, still there in August, 1969.

Dimensions: Height 58.5 cm., width (of shaft) 24.5 cm., thickness of shaft 17 cm.

> Bibliography: Fontrier, *Mouseion kai Bibliotheke*, V, ii, 1886, p. 82, no. φοδ'; Drexler, *op. cit.*, col. 2704, no. 19; Smirnoff, *op. cit.*, p. 98, no. 34; Perdrizet, *op. cit.*, p. 58, top, no. 5; Lane, I, p. 17, note 49.

The stone bears the following inscription:

Μητρὶ Ἀτίμιτι
καὶ Μηνὶ Τιάμ-
ου Γλύκων
Τρύφωνος καὶ
Τρόφιμος Θεο-
γένου κατ' ἐπι-
ταγὴν τὸν βωμ-
ὸν ἐκ τῶν ἰδίων
ἀνέθηκαν.

50. Marble stele first seen in Ayazviran in 1969, in a house belonging to Mehmet Çiçek.

Dimensions: Height 88 cm., width at bottom 50.5 cm., width at narrowest point under pediment, 40.5 cm., thickness ca. 4 cm., letters ca. 1.5 cm.

Bibliography: Lane, *AS*, XX, 1970, pp. 51-52 and Pl. VIb.

The stele has a round pediment, within which there is a crescent moon in relief. The main area of the stele is occupied, at the top, by a representation in relief, and at the bottom, by an inscription. In spite of some irregularity at the bottom, the stele appears complete. It was apparently broken in antiquity by a fissure running across the relief field from the upper left to the lower right, and was repaired, likewise in antiquity, by two lead dowels still fixed in the lower part.

The relief portrays, on the viewer's left, the god Men standing frontally, wearing his usual long tunic, chiton with long sleeves, and boots. On his head there is the usual Phrygian cap, its point bent to the viewer's left and spilling over onto the diagonal surface that spreads out to support the pediment. In his right hand, Men holds an indistinct round object, perhaps a pine-cone, and in his left a spear with a large, broad point. On either side of his feet, two miniature lions face the viewer frontally. The round eyes and small mouths, on the face of Men as well as on those of the lions, lend them a charmingly naive expression. The right portion of the relief is occupied by a humped bull, intermediate in scale between Men and the lions, who with his tail in the air and his face turned toward the viewer, seems almost to come skipping up to Men and is entirely in line with the generally humorous tone of the composition.

The inscription under the relief reads as follows:

Μηνὶ Ἀξιοττηνῷ. Τατιανὴ Ἐρ-　　　235-6 A.D.
που εὐξαμένη ταῦρον ὑ-
πὲρ ἀδελφῶν καὶ ἀκουσ-
θεῖσα, μὴ δυνασθεῖσα δὲ
ἀποδοῦναι ταῦρον, ἠρώτη-
σε τὸν θεὸν καὶ συνεχώρησε
ἀπολαβεῖν στήλλην. Ἔτους τκ´,
μη(νὸς) Πανήμου ι´.

Aivatlar, Turkey (area of Kula)

51. Marble stele with projecting moulding on top. Found by Kurtoğlu Haci Seraphion at Aivatlar ca. 1885, and brought by him to Gyölde.

```
(TWO LINES ERASED)

          ϚΝΚΑΙΙ·ΙΔΥ
        ΑιΙΟΛΛΩΝΙΟΣ
        ΤΟ·ΑΠΟΛΛΩΝΙ
        ΟΥ·✱Μ̃·ΕΙΤΑΑΠΑ
    ΙΟΥΝΤΟΣ ΤΟΥΑΠΟΛΛΩΝΙΟΥΤΟΝΧΑΛ
    ΚΟΝΠΑΡΑΤΟΥΣΚΟΛΛΟΥΩΜΟΣΕΤΟΥΣ
    ΠΡΟΓΕΓΡΑΜΕΝΟΥΣΘΕΟΥΣΙΣΠΡΟ
    ΘΕΣΜΙΑΝΑΠΟΔΟΥΝΑΙΤΟΣΥΝΑ
    ΧΘΕΝΚΕΦΑΛΑΙΟΝΜΙ·ΤΙ·ΡΙ·ΙΣΑΝΤΟΣ
    ΑΥΤΟΥΤΙ·ΙΝΠΙΣΤΙΝΠΑΡΕΧΩΡΙ·ΙΣΕΝ
    ΤΙ·ΘΕΩΟΑΠΟΛΛΩΝΙΟΣΚΟΛΛΣΘΕΝ
    ΤΟΣΟΥΝΤΟΥΣΚΟΛΛΟΥΥΠΟΤΩΝΘΓ
    ΩΝΙΣΘΑΝΑΤΟΥΛΟΓΟΝΜΕΤΑΤΙ·ΙΝ
    ΛΕΥΤΙ·ΙΝΑΥΤΟΥΕΠΕΖΙ·ΙΤΙ·ΘΙ·ΙΥΠΟΤ
    ΘΕ·ΩΝ ΤΑΤΙΑΣΟΥΝΙ·ΙΘΥΓΑΤΙ·ΙΡΑΥΤΟΥ
    ΕΛΟΙΣΕΤΟΥΣΟΡΚΟΥΣΚΑΙΝΥΝΕΙΛΑ
    ΣΑΜΕΝΙ·ΙΕΥΛΟΓΕΙΜΙ·ΙΤΡΙΑΤΙΜΙΤΙ
    ΚΑΙΜΙ·ΙΝΙΤΙΑΜΟΥ - ΕΤΟΥΣ̄ - ΣΤ̄·ΜΜ
    ΞΑΝΝΔΙΚΟΥ·ΕΪ
```

No. 51

Dimensions: Height 78 cm., width 38-40 cm., thickness 4 cm.

Bibliography: Drexler, *op. cit.*, col. 2703-4, no. 18; *Mouseion kai Bibliotheke*, V, ii, 1885-6, p. 84-5, no. φοζ'; Ramsay, *JHS*, X, 1889, p. 227, note 2; Smirnoff, *op. cit.*, pp. 97-8, no. 32; Perdrizet, *op. cit.*, p. 59, no. 3; K.P, II Reise, p. 107; Steinleitner, *op. cit.*, no. 6; Buckler, *ABSA*, XXI, 1914-16, pp. 175-80, no. 4; Lane, I, p. 17, no. 16.

The stone bears the following inscription of which the first two lines and part of the next four are illegible. Buckler's restoration follows:

[Μεγάλη Μήτηρ Ἄτιμις]   118-9 A.D.
[καὶ μέγας Μὴν Τιάμου τὴν ···]
[··· κώμην βασιλεύ]ων καὶ ἡ δύ-
[ναμις αὐτῶν μεγάλη.] Ἀπολλώνιος
[Σκόλλῳ παρέθε]το Ἀπολλωνί-
ῳ [ὑπάρχοντα χαλκ]οῦ ✱ μ(ύρια). Εἶτα ἀπα(ι)-
τοῦντος τοῦ Ἀπολλωνίου τὸν χαλ-
κὸν παρὰ τοῦ Σκόλλου ὤμοσε τοὺς
προγεγραμ(μ)ένους θεοὺς ἰς προ-
θεσμίαν ἀποδοῦναι τὸ
συναχθὲν κεφάλαιον. Μὴ τηρήσαντος
αὐτοῦ τὴν πίστιν παρεχώρησεν
τῇ θεῷ ὁ Ἀπολλώνιος. Κολασθέν-
τος οὖν τοῦ Σκόλλου ὑπὸ τῶν θεῶν ἰς θανάτου λόγον μετὰ τὴν [τε-]
λευτὴν αὐτοῦ ἐπεζητήθη ὑπὸ τ[ῶν]
θεῶν. Τατιὰς οὖν ἡ θυγάτηρ αὐτοῦ
ἔλοισε τοὺς ὅρκους καὶ νῦν εἰλα-
σαμένη εὐλογεῖ Μητρὶ Ἀτίμιτι
καὶ Μηνὶ Τιάμου. Ἔτουσ σγ', μη(νὸς)
Ξανδικοῦ ει'.

(✱ = δηνάρια)

Maeonia: Menye, Turkey (area of Kula)

52. Plaque built into a fountain in Menye. Discovered before 1870.

Dimensions unknown.

Bibliography: Le Bas-Waddington, *op. cit.*, III, i, p. 214, no. 675; Drexler, *op. cit.*, col. 2702, no. 8; Lane, I, p. 15, Lydia no. 6.

The stone bears the following enigmatic inscription, as copied:

Μ[ηνὶ] Ὁσήῳ Μάνης καὶ Βάνας ὁ
Μ[· · · · · ·]λλιωλιας ἡ μήτηρ αὐτῶν
τὸ πρόπυλον ειι ον

53. Stele of marble with relief and inscription, known at least since 1829, brought to Kula from Menye.
Dimensions unknown.

Bibliography: *CIG*, 3439; Keppel, *op. cit.*, II, p. 351, no. 6; C. Texier, *Description de l'Asie Mineure*, Paris, 1850, I, p. 135, Pl. 51 top; *Wagener, *Inscriptions grecques recueillies en Asie Mineure*, Mémoires de l'Académie de Belgique, XXX, p. 5; Le Bas-Waddington, *op. cit.*, III, i, p. 213, no. 668; Le Bas-Reinach, *Planches* to preceding work, Paris, 1888, p. 117 f., Mon. fig., Plate 136, no. 1; Daremberg-Saglio, III, ii, p. 1393, fig. 4662; Drexler, *op. cit.*, co. 2702, no. 13; W. H. Roscher, *Akademie der Wissenschaften, Leipzig, Phil.-Hist. Klasse, Berichte*, XLIII, 1891, p. 125 c, Pl. II bottom; Perdrizet, *op. cit.*, p. 60, no. 2; A. B. Cook, *Zeus*, Cambridge, 1913-40, I, p. 193, fig. 142; M. J. Vermaseren, *Vigiliae Christianae*, IV, 1950, pp. 142-156; Lane, I, p. 16, no. 11.

The stone has a relief portraying a bust of a youthful sun-god, left, and a bust of Men with crescent and Phrygian (?) cap, right, on a projecting ledge. Under the relief there is the following inscription:

Κατὰ τὴν τῶν θεῶν ἐπιτα-   171-172 A.D.
γὴν ἱερὸς δοῦμος εὐχὴν
Διὶ Μασφαλατηνῷ καὶ Μηνὶ
Τιάμου καὶ Μηνὶ Τυράννῳ
ἐκέλευσεν τηρεῖσθαι ἀ-
πὸ ἡμερῶν θ'. Εἴ τις δὲ τούτων ἀπειθήσι, ἀναγνώσ-
εται τὰς δυνάμις τοῦ Δι-
ὸς. Ἐπιμελησαμένου
Διονυσίου, Διοδώρου,
καὶ Ἑρμογένους Βαλερίου,
ἔτους σνς', μη(νὸς) Δύστρου.

ΚΑΤΑ ΤΙΝ ΤΩΝ ΘΕΩΝ ΕΠΙΤΑ
ΓΗΝ ΙΕΡΟΣ ΔΟΥΜΟΣ ΕΥΧΙΝ
ΔΙ ΙΜ ΑΣΦΑΛΑΤΗΝ ΩΚΑΙ ΜΗΝ
ΤΙΑΜΟΥ ΚΑΙ ΜΗΝΙ ΤΥΡΑΝΝΩ
ΕΚΕΛΕΥΣΕΝ ΤΕΡΕΙΣΘΑΙ Α
ΠΟΗΜΕΡΟΝ ΘΕΙ ΤΙΣ ΔΕ ΤΟΥ
ΤΩΝ ΑΠΕΙΘΗΣΙ ΑΝΑΓΝΩΣ
ΕΤΑΙ ΤΑΣ ΔΥΝΑΜΙΣ ΤΟΥ ΔΙ
ΟΣ ΕΠΙΜΕΛΗΣΑΜΕΝΟΥ
ΔΙΟΝΥΣΙΟΥ ΔΙΟΔΩΡΟΥ
ΚΑΙ ΕΡΜΟΓΕΝΟΥΣ ΒΑΛΕΡΙΟΥ
ΕΤΟΥΣ ΣΝϚ Μ. ΔΥΣΤΡΟΥ

No. 53

No. 54

54. Stele in Kula, brought from Menye and known at least since 1829, with relief and inscription.

Dimensions unknown.

> Bibliography: *CIG*, 3438; Keppel, *op. cit.*, II, p. 349-50, no. 5; Texier, *op. cit.*, p. 136, Pl. 52; Le Bas-Waddington, *op. cit.*, III, i, p. 212, no. 667; Daremberg-Saglio, III, ii, p. 1384, fig. 4665; P. Foucart, *BCH*, IV, 1880, p. 129; Drexler, *op. cit.*, col. 2703, no. 14; Leemans, *op. cit.*, p. 38; Le Bas-Reinach, *op. cit.*, p. 118, Mon. fig. Pl. 136, no. 2; Roscher, *op. cit.*, p. 125 d and Pl. II top; Perdrizet, *op. cit.*, p. 60, no. 1; F. Cumont, *Textes et monuments figurés relatifs aux mystères de Mithra*, Brussels 1899, II, p. 220, fig. 50; A. B. Cook, *Zeus*, I, p. 731, fig. 540; Vermaseren, *Vigiliae Christianae*, IV, 1950, pp. 142-156; Herrmann, *op. cit.*, p. 43; Lane, I, p. 16, no. 12.

The stone bears a relief-field at the top, which shows Men on left, standing with crescent, Phrygian cap, and usual costume, holding a spear in his right hand, a pine-cone (?) in his left, his left foot on the head of a prostrate bull, which stretches from the left margin of the relief field behind Men's right leg to lay its head in the proper position. To the right there is an aged Zeus Masphalatenos, holding an eagle in his outstretched right hand, a short staff in his left. Under the relief there is the following inscription:

Ἱερὰ συμβίωσις καὶ νεωτέρα κατ' ἐπι-   171-172 A.D.
ταγὴν τοῦ κοιρίου τυράννου Διὸς Μασ-
φαλατηνοῦ καὶ Μηνὶ Τιάμου εὐχήν. Ἰουλ(ι)-
ανὸς Μενεκράτου, Μενεκράτης Διοδώρου, Διονοίσιος Παπίου, Ἑρμογένης Ἑρμίππου, Λούκιος Ὀνησίμου, Διογένης
Γλύκωνος, Διογένης Μαξίμου, Τρόφιμο[ς]
Ἑρμίππου, Ἀπολλώνιος β', Θεόδωρος β',
Μαρκιανὸς β', Μένανδρος Ἑρμογένου, Ἑρμογένης Στατιανοῦ, Μητρόδωρος Εὐελπίσ-
του, Ἀσκληπιάδης Μαρκιανοῦ, Ἀσκληπιάδης Διονοισίου, Ἑρμογένης Τροφίμου,
Βάβηλος Ἑρμογένου, ἐπιμελησαμένων
Ἰουλιανοῦ καὶ Ἑρμογένου. Ἔτους σνς', μη(νὸς) Δ(ύστρου).

55. Fragmentary stele of white marble, broken above, below, right. Menye, in house of Süleyman Türe. Known since before 1962.

Dimensions: Height 33 cm., width 30 cm., thickness 4.5 cm., height of letters 1.5 cm.

Bibliography: Herrmann, *op. cit.*, p. 48-9, no. 42, Pl. XIII, no. 3; Robert, *REG*, LXXVI, 1963, p. 168, no. 227; Lane, I, p. 51, no. A8.

The stone bears the following inscription:

172-3 A.D.

[Ἔτου]ς σγζ', μη(νὸς) Πανήμ[ου·· Ἐπεὶ]
Ἕρμιππος Ἑρμίππου [···············]
σετο τὸν θεὸν Μῆνα ΚΓ[··············]
μετὰ τῶν ἰδίων ἀδε[λφῶν Διονυσίου, Ἀ-]
πολλωνίου, Ὀρφέος ἀ[πέκτεινε ·········]
τὸν ἐπιζητηθέντα [···············μετὰ]
Διονυσίου τοῦ ἀδελ[φοῦ············μετὰ]
τὸ τετελευτηκένα[ι αὐτοὺς ············]

ASIA MINOR

εἱλάσαντο τὸν θεὸν [καὶ ἀπὸ νῦν εὐλο-]
γοῦσιν.

(Herrmann's conjectural restoration)

Görnevit, Turkey (area of Kula)

56. Fragment of marble built into outer wall of house, known since 1893.
Dimensions unknown.

> Bibliography: Buresch, *Reisebericht II*, p. 96f.; *Aus Lydien*, p. 85, no. 41; Lane, I, p. 18, no. 23.

The stone bears the following inscription according to Buresch's restoration. (Kamareites is known as a by-name of Men from coins of Nysa.)

[Μηνὶ Καμα-]   66-67 A.D.
ρείτῃ ε[ὐχὴν]
Ἡρακλείδης Με-
νεκράτους,
ἔτους ρνα′, μη-
νὸς Γορπιαίου
ἀνέθηκεν.

57. Stele of white marble with pediment, broken at bottom, known since 1962.
Dimensions: Height 30 cm., width 28 cm., thickness 4.5 cm., height of letters 1.7 cm.

> Bibliography: Herrmann, *op. cit.*, p. 39, no. 27, Pl. IX, no. 6; Robert, *REG*, LXXVI, 1963, p. 167, no. 225; Lane, I, p. 51, no. A3.

The stone bears the following inscription:

Ἀρτέμιδι Ἀνάειτι
καὶ Μηνὶ Τιάμου Ἀ-
λέξανδρος Τειμό-
θεος Γλύκων τῶν
Βολλάδος καὶ οἱ συν-

βωλαφόροι ἐγλυτρω-
[σάμεν]οι ἀνέστη-
[σαν..........]

Coloe: Kula, Turkey

58. A tablet from Kula, known since at least 1829.
Dimensions unknown.

>Bibliography: *CIG*, 3442; Keppel, *op. cit.*, II, p. 346, no. 1; W. J. Hamilton, *Researches in Asia Minor, Pontus, and Armenia*, 1842, II, p. 467-8, no. 340; Drexler, *op. cit.*, col. 2701, no. 5; S. Reinach, *Traité d'épigraphie grecque*, Paris, 1885, p. 152, note 2; Perdrizet, *op. cit.*, p. 58, bottom, no. 1; Steinleitner, *op. cit.*, p. 34, no. 10; Lane, I, p. 15, Lydia, no. 5.

The stone bears a crescent in relief and under it the following inscription:

[Μ]ηνὶ Ἀξιοττ(η)νῷ. Ἐπὶ
Ἑρμογένης Γλώκωνος
καὶ Νιτωνὶς Φιλοξένου
ἐλοιδώρησαν Ἀρτεμί-
δωρον περὶ οἴνου, Ἀρτε-
μίδωρος πιττάκιον ἔ-
δωκεν. Ὁ θεὸς ἐκολά-
σετο τὸν Ἑρμογένην
καὶ εἰλάσετο τὸν θε-
ὸν καὶ ἀπὸ νῦν εὐδο-
ξεῖ.

59. Plaque of marble discovered in Kula ca. 1880.
Dimensions: Height 18 cm., width 30 cm., thickness 4 cm.

>Bibliography: *Mouseion kai Bibliotheke*, III, 1-2, 1880, p. 127, no. 165; Foucart, *BCH*, IV, 1880, p. 128; Drexler, *op. cit.*, col. 2703, no. 15; Reinach, *RA*, 1885, II, p. 107 and 1886, I, p. 156; Leemans, *op. cit.*, p. 39; Perdrizet, *op. cit.*, p. 58, middle, no. 1; Dittenberger, *SIG*[3], no. 1142; Lane, I, p. 17, no. 13.

The stone bears a relief of two feet, and under them the inscription:

'Αρτέμιδι 'Ανάειτι καὶ
Μηνὶ Τιάμου Μελτίνη
[ὑ]πὲρ τῆς ὁλοκληρίας
[τῶν] ποδῶν εὐχὴν
[ἀνέσ]τησεν.

60. Plaque of marble from Kula, known since 1881, now in Leiden. Broken at top.

Dimensions: Height 48.5 cm., width at top 27.5 cm., width at bottom 36.2 cm., thickness 4.0 cm.

> Bibliography: Drexler, *op. cit.*, col. 2703, no. 17; Leemans, *op. cit.*, p. 8-9, no. 3 and Pl. I, no. 3; Kontoleon, *AM*, XII, 1887, p. 255, no. 19; Polak, *Mnemosyne*, XV, 1887, p. 252ff., no. 3; Hicks, *Classical Review*, III, 1889, p. 69, no. 1; Perdrizet, *op. cit.*, p. 57, no. 2; H. W. Pleket, *Greek Inscriptions in the Rijksmuseum van Oudheden*, Pl. XIV and Appendix II, no. 3; Lane, I, p. 17, no. 15.

The stone has a relief of a woman praying on a projecting ledge and the inscription:

Θεᾷ 'Ανάειτι καὶ Μηνὶ Τιάμου
Μελτίνη καὶ Γλύκων ἀπέδω-
καν τὸ ἱεροποίημα εὐχαρισ-
τοῦντες. Ἔτους τ', μη(νὸς) Ξανδικοῦ.

215-216 A.D.

61. Plaque, located in 1880 in the house of *kyria Barbara* in Kula. In 1901, transported to Smyrna, in the house of the late Dr. Michael Kossagis.

Dimensions: 45 cm. × 40 cm. × 5 cm.

> Bibliography: *Mouseion kai Bibliotheke*, III, i-ii, 1880, p. 162, no. τκς'; Drexler, *op. cit.*, col. 2704, no. 20; W. Fröhner, *Philologus*, Supplement V, 1889, p. 26, no. 25; Ramsay, *JHS*, X, 1889, p. 227, no. 24; Perdrizet, *op. cit.*, p. 57, no. 1; Buresch, *Aus Lydien*, p. 87; Kontoleon, *REG*, XIV, 1901, p. 302, no. 2; Steinleitner, *op. cit.*, p. 36, no. 11; Zingerle, *op. cit.*, col. 26, note 10; Herrmann, *op. cit.*, p. 47; Robert, *REG*, LXXVI, 1963, p. 168, no. 227; Lane, I, p. 17, no. 17.

The stone bears the following inscription:

[Ἔτ]ους σκζ', 'Αρτεμίδω[ρο-]
ς Διοδότου καὶ 'Αμιὰς

μετὰ τῶν συγγενῶν ἐξ ἰδό-
των καὶ μὴ ἰδότων λύτρ-
ον κατ' ἐπιταγὴν Μηνὶ
Τυράννῳ καὶ Διὶ Ὀγμην-
ῷ καὶ τοῖς σὺν αὐτῷ θεοῖς.   142-143 A.D.

62. Plaque found before 1880 at 2 hours distance (on foot?) from Kula. (Probably Kavakh, Steinleitner) Transferred to *Evangelike Schole*, Smyrna.

Dimensions: Height 96 cm., width 58 cm., height of letters 2 cm.

Bibliography: *Mouseion kai Bibliotheke*, III, 1-2, 1880, p. 158, no. τις'; A. Papadopoulos-Kerameus, *AM*, VI, 1881, p. 273-4, no. 23; Drexler, *op. cit.*, col. 2702, no. 11; Perdrizet, *op. cit.*, p. 59, no. 2; Steinleitner, *op. cit.*, p. 33, no. 9; Zingerle, *op. cit.*, col. 42; Herrmann, *op. cit.*, p. 51, note 201 and p. 30, note 102; Lane, I, p. 16, no. 9.

The stone bears a relief of a man putting a scepter on an altar, a boy standing behind him. Under the relief there is the following inscription:

Ἔτους σϙε', μη(νὸς) Περειτίου η',
Μηνὶ Πετραείτῃ καὶ Μηνὶ Λα-
βάνῃ Μητροφάνης καὶ Φλαβια-
νὸς οἱ Φιλιππικοῦ καταλειφθ-
έντες ὑπὸ τῶν γονέων ἐν ὀρ-
φανείᾳ καὶ ἐνίων ἀνθρώπων ἐ-
πιβουλευσάντων αὐτοῖς ἐκ τῆ[ς]
κώμης καὶ ἀρόντων ἔνγραφα καὶ ἕτε-
ρα εἴδη ἐκ τῆς οἰκίας αὐτῶν λα-
θραίως, καὶ περισυρομένων αὐτῶν
ὑπὸ δανειστῶν, ἡ Ταζηνῶν κατοι-
κία ἀδοξήσασα ἐπέστησε τὸ
σκῆπτρον τοῖς κακῶς εἰς α(ὐ)τοὺς τ[ι-]
μήσασιν, καὶ ὁ θεὸς ἐξεζήτησεν [καὶ]
ἐκολάσετο καὶ διέφθειρε τοὺς [ἐπι-]
βουλεύσαντας αὐτοῖς ὁ θεὸς
[···]ις ἐστηλλογράφησα[ν]
[······τὰ]ς δυνάμις ὅτι
[··············]τῆς   210-211 A.D.

63. Stele of coarse white marble, found in Kula, in possession of Museum of Fine Arts, Boston, since about 1850. Somewhat broken on right.

Dimensions: Height 72 cm., width 42 cm., thickness 6 cm.

> Bibliography: Drexler, *op. cit.*, col. 2704; **M.F.A.B. 18th Annual Report, 1894*, p. 20; *Archäologischer Anzieger*, IX, 1894, p. 95; Reinach, *RA*, 1894, II, p. 117; Wright, *HSCP*, VI, 1895, p. 56, Pl. II; *Bulletin MFAB*, LVI, 1958, p. 72; Lane, I, pp. 17-18, no. 19.

The stone bears a relief-field showing, left to right, a man, a child, a woman, and a second child, all raising their right hands in adoration, with a projecting ledge under them. Under the relief is the following inscription:

> ᾿Αρτέμιδι ᾿Ανάειτι κ[αὶ Μη-]   196-197 A.D.
> νὶ Τιάμου Μουσαῖς β' [καὶ]
> Καλλιγένεια ἡ σύμβι[ος αὐ-]
> τοῦ ὑπὲρ Μουσαίου το[ῦ υοῦ]
> μαρτυροῦντες τὰς δ[υνά-]
> μις τῶν θεῶν ἀπέδω[καν]
> τὴν εὐχήν. ῎Ετους σπα', [μη(νὸς)]
> Δείου ι'.

64. Terracotta statuette showing a young, fat, naked Men, sitting, crescent at neck, strap (to hold garment?) across chest, cock in right hand, pine-cone in left, flowers (?) in hair. Found in Kula. Once part of Schlumberger's private collection, but not now in Louvre.

Dimensions unknown.

> Bibliography: Schlumberger, *Gazette Archeologique*, VI, 1880, p. 191ff., Pl. XXXII; Drexler, *op. cit.*, col. 2704-5; *Zeitschrift für Numismatik*, XIV, 1888, pp. 375-77; Roscher, *op. cit.*, p. 125, b and Pl. III; Smirnoff, *op. cit.*, p. 119, fig. 3; Perdrizet, *op. cit.*, p. 59; Lane, I, p. 19, no. 29.

65. Stele with round pediment and lug, known since 1962. Dimensions unavailable.

> Bibliography: Herrmann, *op. cit.*, p. 46, no. 39, Pl. XII, no. 1; Robert, *REG*, LXXVI, 1963, p. 168, no. 227; Lane, I, p. 51, no. A5.

The stone bears three reliefs: in pediment, Men, staff in left hand, pine-cone in right, flanked by two lions facing in; in main field a horse and rider going left, groom standing at horse's head. Under the first line of the inscription (which is on a sort of projection), a foot and leg. It also has the following inscription:

Μηνὶ Ἀξιττηνῷ   269-70 A.D.
Ὀνησίμη ἡ μήτηρ ὑπὲρ
τοῦ ὑοῦ Τυράννου, ἐπει-
δὴ τὸν πόδα πονήσας εὐ-
λογοῦσα ἀνέθηκα. Ἔτους
τνδ', μη(νὸς) ϛ' Ξανδικοῦ Θι'.

66. Stele of white marble in 1962 in Kula although perhaps not originally from there. It has a pediment and lug.

Dimensions: Height 80 cm., width 36 cm., thickness 6 cm., height of letters 2 cm.

> Bibliography: Herrmann, *op. cit.*, p. 47, no. 41 and Plate XII, no. 3; Robert, *REG*, LXXVI, 1963, p. 168, no. 227; Lane, I, p. 51, no. A7.

The stone has a relief of Men holding a staff in his right hand and a pine-cone (?) in his left, and under it the following inscription:

Μῆνα ἐγ Διοδότου   148-9 A.D.
Ἀλέξανδρος Θαλού-
σης μετὰ Ἰουλίου καὶ
τῆς ἀδελφῆς ἐλυτρώ-
σαντο τὸν θεὸν ἐξ εἰδό-
των καὶ μὴ εἰδότων.
Ἔτους σλγ'.

Kavaklı, Turkey, (area of Kula)

67. Fragment of a marble stele, in 1898 built into a house wall on the south edge of the village. Still there in 1962.
Dimensions unknown.

> Bibliography: Drexler, *op. cit.*, col. 2702, no. 10; Buresch, *Reisebericht II*, p. 98f.; Perdrizet, *op. cit.*, p. 57, no. 4; Buresch, *Aus Lydien*, p. 111, no. 53; Ramsay, *Classical Review*, XIII, 1899, p. 142; K-P, II Reise,

p. 105; Steinleitner, *op. cit.*, p. 29, no. 8; Rostovzeff, *op. cit.*, p. 656, note 6; Herrmann, *op. cit.*, p. 49, note 197 and Pl. XII, no. 2; Lane, I, p. 16, no. 8.

The stone bears the following inscription, according to Keil and von Premerstein's restoration, under a lost relief, traces of the field for which are discernible:

>   Μέγας   [Μὴν]
>   Πετραείτης [τὴν κώμην βα-]
>   σιλεύων κ(αὶ) μ[εγάλη θεῶν]
>   Μήτηρ Ταζη[νή. Φιλιππι-]
>   κὸς Τατιαυ[οῦ, ἐπειδὴ λύ-]
>   μην ἐποίησ[α ἐπιορκήσας,]
>   ἀπελεγχθε[ὶς ὑπὸ τῶν ἀν-]
>   τιδίκων νῦ[ν ἱλασάμενος]
>   μετὰ υἱοῦ [ἐστηλλογρά-]
>   φησα τὰς δ[υνάμεις ὑμῶν]
>   Ἔτους σ[···ʹ, μη(νὸς)···]
>   ου ηʹ.

68. Stele of white marble, broken at top. Found before 1962 in front of house door of Veli Çalık. Damaged left surface.

Dimensions: Height 40 cm., width 45 cm., thickness 7 cm., height of letters 2.5 cm.

>   Bibliography: Herrmann, *op. cit.*, p. 49, no. 43, Plate XIII, no. 2; Robert, *REG*, LXXVI, 1963, p. 168, no. 227; Lane, I, p. 52, no. A9.

The stone bears the following inscription:

>   [Ἔτ]ους τγιʹ, μ[η(νὸς)···]
>   [·]ονις ὑπὲρ Μάρκου τοῦ
>   [ὑ]οῦ εὐξαμένη Μηνὶ
>   [Π]ετραείτῃ εὐλογῶ.

Tarsi?: Köleköy, Turkey, (area of Kula)
(including area towards Kalburcu)

69. Stele of white marble supposedly found 1 km. south of village before 1962. Moulding at top, lug at bottom.

Dimensions: Height 1.00 m., width 48 cm., thickness 7 cm., height of letters 1.5 cm.

> Bibliography: Herrmann, *op. cit.*, p. 30, no. 21, Plate VIII, no. 2; Robert, *REG*, LXXVI, 1963, p. 170, no. 235; Lane, I, p. 50, no. A2.

The stone bears a relief showing Men holding staff on right, pine-cone on left, beside him to viewer's left a piece of clothing, and underneath, to the left, a boy with uplifted hands. After the relief there is the following inscription:

Μέγας Μεὶς Ἀξιοττηνὸς Τάρσι βα-   164-5 A.D.
σιλεύων. Ἐπεὶ ἐπεστάθη σκῆ-
πτρον εἴ τις ἐκ τοῦ βαλανείου τι
κλέψι, κλαπέντος οὖν εἱματίου
ὁ θεὸς ἐνεμέσησε τὸν κλέπτην
καὶ ἐπόησε μετὰ χρόνον τὸ εἱμά-
τιον ἐνενκῖν ἐπὶ τὸν θεὸν καὶ ἐ-
ξωμολογήσατο. Ὁ θεὸς οὖν ἐκέλευ-
σε δἰ ἀνγέλου πραθῆναι τὸ εἱμά-
τιν καὶ στηλλογραφῆσαι τὰς δυνάμεις. Ἔτους σμθ'.

70. Funerary stele with pediment and lug at bottom, found on farm of Mustafa Filik between Kalburcu and Köleköy. Known since 1962.

Dimensions: Height 88 cm., width 38 cm., thickness 6 cm., height of letters 1.2 cm.

> Bibliography: Herrmann, *op. cit.*, p. 58-9, no. 53, Plate XV, no. 4; Robert, *REG*, LXXVI, 1963, p. 168, no. 233; Lane, I, p. 52, no. A11.

There is a relief portraying a wreath followed by an inscription:

Ἔτους ρπγ', μη(νὸς) Πανήμου   98-9 A.D.
ς', Δημήτριος Τειμάου καὶ
Ἀμμία ἡ γυνὴ αὐτοῦ Δη-
μόφιλον τὸν ἑαυτῶν υἱ-
ὸν καὶ Ζηνᾶς ὁ ἀδελφὸς
αὐτοῦ ἐτείμησαν. Εἰ δέ
τις προσαμαρτάνῃ τῷ μνημεί-
ῳ, τεύξηται τοῦ Ἀξιοττη-
νοῦ κεχολωμένου.

71. Funerary stele of white marble with pediment and lug found in same place as preceding. Known since 1962.

Dimensions: Height 1.10 m., width 39 cm., thickness 9 cm., height of letters 1.2 cm.

> Bibliography: Herrmann, *op. cit.*, p. 59, no. 55, Plate XVI, no. 3; Robert, *REG*, LXXVI, 1963, p. 168, no. 233; Lane, I, p. 52, no. A12.

There is a relief portraying a wreath, followed by this inscription:

```
Ἔτους ροη', μη(νὸς) Δείου δ',           93-4 A.D.
Ἀμιὰς ἡ γυνὴ καὶ οἱ υἱοὶ
Ἀπολλώνιος καὶ Δημό-
φιλος ἐτείμησαν Πατερῇ
καὶ Τρύφαινα ἡ θρεπτή.
Ἵνα μή τις προσαμάρτῃ τῇ
στήλῃ ἢ τῷ μνημείῳ, σκῆ-
πτρα ἐπέστησαν τοῦ Ἀξ[ι-]
οττηνοῦ καὶ Ἀναείτιδος.
```

Karaoba (or Fülöz), Turkey (area of Kula)
(Fölüz on map) [1]

72. Block of white marble high in the wall of house of Halil Çıldır. Known since 1962.

Dimensions: Height 40 cm., width 25 cm., height of letters 1.5 cm. approximate.

> Bibliography: Herrmann, *op. cit.*, p. 45, no. 38; Robert, *REG*, LXXVI, 1963, p. 167-8, no. 227; Lane, I, p. 51, no. 38.

The stone bears the following inscription:

```
Εὔτυχος Ἰου-
λίας Ταβίλλης
δοῦλος πραγμα-
τευτὴς σὺν
καὶ τῇ γυναικὶ
Ἐπιγόνῃ εὐχὴν
ὑπὲρ υἱοῦ Νεικη-
```

[1] References to the map are to the Turkish army survey map of Turkey.

[τ]ου Μηνὶ Ἀξι-
εττηνῷ διὰ
τὸ σωθῆναι αὐ-
τὸν ὑπὸ τοῦ θε-
οῦ ἀσθενοῦντα.

Kavacık, Turkey (area of Kula)

73. Small round altar of white marble. Known since 1962. Dimensions: Height 33 cm., diameter 16-18 cm.

> Bibliography: Herrmann, *op. cit.*, p. 50, no. 44, Plate XII, no. 4; Robert, *REG*, LXXVI, 1963, p. 168, no. 227; Lane, I, p. 52, no. A11.

There is a relief of a crescent moon, followed by the inscription:

Μηνὶ Τιά-
μου Φρό-
νιμος
εὐχήν.

General area of Kula, exact provenience unknown

74. Stele of white marble with pediment, in the middle of which there is a round object, and acroteria. Entered into museum of Manisa between 1948 and 1954. Since—with only one exception—Men Tiamou is known only from the area of Kula, this item can also be ascribed to it.

Dimensions: Height 45 cm., width at bottom 29 cm., height of letters 1.5 cm.

> Bibliography: L. Robert, *Hellenica*, X, 1955, p. 163 and Plate 29, no. 1; Lane, I, p. 19, no. 28.

The main field of the stone carries a relief of two breasts, and the following inscription:

Ἀρτέμιδι Ἀνάε[ιτι]
καὶ Μηνὶ Τιάμου Ἀ[λε-]
ξάνδρα ὑπὲρ τῶν

μαστῶν εὐχὴν
ἀνέστησαν.

Darmara, Turkey

75. Stone of unknown type originally from Darmara [but according to *REG* found shortly before 1892 in Baindir (= Bayindir)], in 1895 built into the church *ton taxiarchon* in Tire. Dimensions unknown.

Bibliography: Drexler, *op. cit.*, col. 2708; Kontoleon, *REG*, V, 1892, p. 341; T. Homolle, *BCH*, XVIII, 1894, p. 539; *AM*, XX, 1895, p. 242; *Buresch, *Harmonia*, 1 and 12 April, 1895; K-P, II Reise, p.175; Lane, I, p. 21, no. 30.

The stone bears the following inscription:

OM
Π(όπλιον) Αἴλιον Μενεκράτην
τῇ ἱερείᾳ τῆς Δήμητρος
ἀνενένκαντα καὶ καθιερώ-
σαντα κάλαθον περιάργυρον
τὸν λείποντα τοῖς τῆς Δήμητρος μυστηρίοις, καὶ τῷ προκα-
θημένῳ τῆς κώμης Μηνὶ ση-
μήαν περιάργυρον, τὴν προ-
πομπεύουσαν τῶν μυστηρί-
ων αὐτοῦ. Διά τε τοῦτο καθι-
έρωσεν ὑπὲρ τῆς ἱεροσύνης
εἰς τὰς ἐπιθυσίας τῆς Δήμητρος τὰ πρὸ τῆς οἰκίας ἐργα-
στήρια εἰς τὸ κατ' ἐνιαυτὸν
ἕκαστον τῇ τοῦ καλάθου
ἀναφορᾷ τοὺς κληρωθέν-
τας εἰς τὴν πομπὴν ἄνδρας
μετὰ τῶν ἀρχόντων προθύ-
οντας εὐωχεῖσθαι ἐν τῇ
οἰκίᾳ αὐτοῦ διὰ παντὸς τοῦ
βίου.

Ἐπὶ ἄρχοντος τῆς κατοικίας
Βερίου Βάσσου φιλοσεβάστου καὶ
τῶν συναρχόντων αὐτοῦ.

Mostene (?): Assar Tepe, near Kassaba (Turgutlu),
Turkey (RR Sta. Urgamlı on Hermus)

76. A stone of unknown type found about 1895, and subsequently sent to the Turkish School Mehkel-Idadie in Smyrna. (Inquiries in 1969 fail to reveal any knowledge of this school's existence.) Dimensions unknown.

Bibliography: T. Homolle, *op. cit.*, p. 542; *AM*, XX, 1895, p. 501; *Buresch, *Harmonia*, May 12, 1895; Lane, I, p. 21, no. 31.

The stone bears the following, largely enigmatic, inscription:

[・・・・・・・・・・・・・・]νος ἔδωκεν ἡμεῖν [τὸ・・・・・・・・・・・・・]
[・・・・・・・・・・・・・・]οις ἀνθρώποις συνοχῆς[・・・・・・・・・・・]
[・・・・・・・・・・・・・・]αν ὥραν ἡμεῖν ὧν ἐπέταξεν [θεὸς・・・]
[・・・・・・・・・・・・・・]ωμεν μὲν Μηνὸς καὶ Διὸς καὶ Κ[・・・・]
[・・・・・・・・・・κ]αὶ τῶν κρατούντων θεῶν Σεβα[στῶν・・・・・]
[・・・・・・・・・・・・]ήσπισεν ἄνθρωπος ὑπὸ θεῶν[・・・・・・・・・・・]
[・・・・・・・・・・・・]όσοις βωμοῖς καὶ [χ]άριν ἔσχεν οἷς σ[・・]
[・・・・・・・・・・・κ]αὶ Μηνογένης Βούτας ο[ἱ・・・・・・・・・・・・・・]
[・・・・・・・・・τ]οῖς ἰδίοις μηδὲν ἐνλείπων κα[ὶ・・・・・・・・・・]
[・・・・・・・・・ι]κῆς, ἧς καὶ μαντοσύνη κέκληται ὑπὸ θεῶ[ν]
[・・・・・・]α ἐνέργειαν περὶ (τ)ῆς κατοικίας καὶ τῶν κρατούντω[ν],
     ὡς ἐπέταξεν θεὸς προκαλούμενος ἀνθρώπ[οις]
εὐσέβηαν ἵν' ἔχωσιν τὸ[ν] τόπον ἀσπίζειν προσκυ[νοῦντες]
[・・]μασιν νέμεσθαι, περὶ ὧν ἐπέταξεν θεός, καὶ μηδέν[α]
ἀνθρώπων ἀντιπεσεῖν τῷδε τόπῳ τ[ῶ]ν κρατού[ντων]
τῶν ἐπὶ τὴν βασίληαν κήπ[ω]ν, φυτῶν, εὐχόρτων π[εδίων]
[・・・]μοντα ὥσπερ Ἀφροδίτης, ὃν συνανέστησεν θ[εὸς]
πρόπυλον ἀριλλῶν σὺν κοσμήμασιν καὶ δένδρ[οις]
[・・・]σιν οἷς ἀπέδωκεν θεὸς ἀνθρώποις. Ταῦτ' ἐπ[・・・]
σωφροσύνῃ ἀρκετὸν ἤδη γράμμα χαρὰν (π)αρέχον.

Sardis: Sart, Turkey

77. Slab of bluish marble, broken on all sides (part of right edge preserved, but not surface), brought in 1910 from a house in the village to the museum.

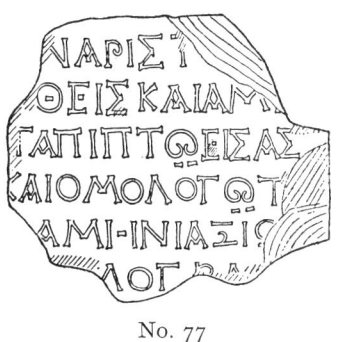

No. 77

Dimensions: Height 19 cm., width 22.5 cm., height of letters 1.7 cm.

> Bibliography: Keil and von Premerstein, *Bericht über eine Reise in Lydien* (hereafter, K-P, I Reise), Öst. Ak. der Wiss., Denkschriften, Phil.-Hist. Klasse, LIII, ii, 1907, pp. 15-16, no. 25; Steinleitner, *op. cit.*, p. 46, no. 20; *Sardis*, VII, i ,Leiden, 1932, p. 98, no. 96; Lane, I, p. 21, no. 32.

The stone bears the following inscription:

[····ω]ν Ἀριστ[ονεί-]
[κου ἐλεη]θεὶς καὶ ἀμ[αρ-]
[τήσας κα]ταπίπτω εἰς ἀ[σ-]
[θένειαν] καὶ ὁμολογῶ τ[ὸ]
[ἁμάτρημ]α Μηνὶ Ἀξιω[τ-]
[τηνῷ καὶ στη]λογρ[αφῶ].

78. Fragmentary marble stele with relief from a field at Sardis, found ca. 1880 by Dr. Magrath, now in Ashmolean Museum, Oxford.

Dimensions: Height 22.5 cm., width 21 cm., thickness 5 cm. Broken on all sides except possibly the base.

> Bibliography: *Sardis*, VII, i, p. 98, no. 96a; Lane, I, p. 22, no. 32a.

Men is portrayed riding right, facing the viewer slightly, towards a small altar. He has a crescent at his neck, but it is uncertain whether he has any headdress. His right hand may be holding a short stick, his left is hidden behind the horse's neck. The horse has his left foreleg raised, the right on the ground.

79. Slab of stone seen in Sardis in 1874 and moved thence to Smyrna RR Sta. in 1876-8; present whereabouts unknown.
Dimensions: Height 1.10 m., width 65 cm., thickness 14 cm.

> Bibliography: Frontrier, *Mouseion kai Bibliotheke*, II, 2-3, 1876-8, p. 25; Drexler, *op. cit.*, col. 2707; Perdrizet, *op. cit.*, p. 71, note 1; Sardis, VII, i, pp. 37-40, no. 17; Lane, I, p. 22, no. 34.

The stone bears the following inscription:

καὶ ὅσοις ἀπενεμ[ήθη ὕδωρ: κρήνη]
γυμνασίῳ γερουσι[ακῷ ἐναντία, κρήνη]
μυστηρίοις δυσὶ[ν ἐναντία, κρήνη]
Δομιτίας ⚹ ε′, κρήνη ε[··········]
κρήνη Δηναεῖτ(ις) πρὸς τοῖς [·····]
κρήνη μυστηρίῳ Ἄττει ἐνα[ντία ἀπόρρυ-]
τος εἰς τὸ Διός, συναγωγῆ[ς κρήνη],
κρήνη πρὸς τῷ Ὠδείῳ ⚹ γ′, [κρήνη····]
του πρὸς τῇ διστέγῳ τῆς [····· οὗ καὶ]
πύργοι Δ^Α β′, ἀνδροφυλακί[ου κρήνη ἢ ἐπὶ]
τῇ καθόδῳ ἀγορᾶς πρὸς τ[······· ὕδωρ]
πέμπει, κρήνη ἐν τοῖς [············]
ρίου, ἀπὸ ὑδρείο[υ κρήνη, κρήνη Λυσι-]
μάχου ⚹ γ′, κρήνη π[······· πρὸς τῷ]
Μηνογενείῳ ⚹ γ′, κρή[νη Ἀρσινόης,]
ἀπὸ τῆς Ἀρσινόης κρ[ήνη ἀπόρρυτος]
περὶ τὸ Μηνὸς, κρήνη ἐ[ν··········]
του πρὸς τῇ πύλῃ, κρ[ῆναι ἃς κατεσκεύασαν]
Ῥοῦφος καὶ Λέπιδο[ς·············]
Αὐρηλία Ἰουλία Μηνο[············]
δρα Δ^Α β′, Ἀσίννιος Μ[············]
νος Δ^Α α′, Φλ. Σεχ[··············]

Δ^Α = τετράμφορα
⚹ = ἑκοντάχους

80. Two fragments of a stele of white marble, decreasing in size towards the top. Top piece found in pavement of the "House of Bronzes" in Sardis in 1959, bottom piece in the courtyard of a house in the village in 1961. Now in Sardis excavation collection. The two pieces have been convincingly put together by L. Robert.

Dimensions: Top piece (recut as column base): height 24 cm., width at bottom 33 cm., thickness 5.5 cm., letter height 1.6 to 1.8 mm. Bottom piece, height 42 cm., width at bottom 37.5 cm., width at top 32 cm., thickness 5 to 6 cm., height of letters 1.5 to 2.0 cm.

Bibliography: *Illustrated London News*, July 9, 1960; L. Robert, *Nouvelles Inscriptions de Sardes*, pp. 23-24, nos. 2 and 3 and Plate II, no. 2, Plate III, no. 2; Lane, I, p. 22, no. 33 and II, p. 45, no. 7.

There is an incised crescent moon at the top; after which there follows the inscription, as put together by Robert:

[Μην]ὶ ’Αξιοτηνῷ ’Ε[πα-]   160-161 A.D.
[φρόδ]ειτος οἰκο[νό-]
[μος Κλαυ]δίο[υ Στρα-]
[τ]ονείκου εὐξά[με-]
νος ἐὰν λήψεται
γυναῖκαν ἣν θέλω
καὶ λαβὼν καὶ μὴ ἀ-
ποδὼν τὴν εὐχήν,
κολασθεὶς ἀνέθη-
κεν καὶ ἀπὸ νῦν εὐλο-
γεῖ μετὰ τῶν ἰδίων
πάντων. Ἔτους σμε΄,
μη(νὸς) Δείου βι΄.

81. Marble sepulchral slab, known since 1811. In 1874 "chez le bakkal, Dimitri." Now lost.

Dimensions unknown.

Bibliography: Gardner, *JHS*, VI, 1885, pp. 346-7, no. 76; *Sardis*, VII, i, pp. 127-9, no. 152; L. Robert, *RA*, 1936, I, pp. 238-40; Lane, II, pp. 44-45, no. 6.

The text of the inscription, as restored by Robert, runs as follows:

[··········εἴ τις] δ[έ τινα]

[τῶν προδηλου]μένων ἔξω βάλῃ,
[· · · · · · · · · · ·Μ]ηνὸς Τυμωλεί[του]
[καὶ τῶν θεῶν τ]ῶν ἄλλων πάν[των]
[κεχολωμένων] τύχοιτο μετὰ παν-
[ωλείας πάντ]ων μήτε θρεμμά-
[των ὄνησις εἴ]η μήτε ὀμμάτων
[ὅρασις, αὐτῷ δὲ] ἐξώλη γένοιτο
[καὶ μετὰ θάνα]τον.

Philadelphia Lydiae: Alaşehir, Turkey

82. Pedimental stele of white marble broken at very top. Found before 1908 in pavement of church of St. George, district of Hagia Marina, Alaşehir.

No. 82

Dimensions: Height 50 cm., width 33.5 cm., letter height 2 cm.
Bibliography: K-P, I Reise, p. 27, no. 38; Lane, I, p. 22, no. 35.

In the main field of the stele there is a crescent incised outline *upside down*, and the following inscription:

Σέλευκος Σε-

λεύκου Μηνὶ Τι-
άμου εὐχήν.

Area of *Saittae*: İncikler, Turkey
(Icıklar on map)

83. Altar of whitish marble, mouldings at bottom and top, found before 1911 in front of house of Hacı Hassanoğlu İsmail.

Dimensions: Height 80.5 cm., width 36 cm., height of letters 2.7 to 3.3 cm.

> Bibliography: K-P, II Reise, pp. 109-110, no. 211; Robert, *Anatolia*, III, 1958, p. 128, note 101; Lane, I, p. 22, no. 36.

The stone bears the following inscription:

Εἷς θεὸς ἐ-
ν οὐρανοῖς,
μέγας Μὴν
Οὐράνιος,
μεγάλη δύ-
ναμις τοῦ ἀ-
θανάτου θε-
οῦ.

Magnesia ad Sipylum: Manisa, Turkey

84. Statuette of bronze, found in sanctuary of Meter Plastene east of Manisa, near "statue of Niobe", in 1887. Transported to Constantinople Museum, according to RA article.

Dimensions: Height 50 cm.

> Bibliography: S. Reinach, *RA*, 1887, II, p. 96; A. E. Kontoleon, *AM*, XII, 1887, p. 253, no. 17; Lane, I, p. 22, no. 37.

The statuette represents Men as a rider, and has inscribed on its base:

Μητρὶ θεῶν Πλαστήνῃ
Καλβείσιος Ὀρφεὺς
ἀνέθηκεν.

85. Now in Museum of Manisa. Exact provenience unreported. An altar ca. 3 feet high. Will be fully published by director. The altar bears a decoration of a moon on the front, and on the four corners a ram's head each, connected by garlands. It has the following inscription:

    Μη   νὶ
       moon
    Ἀξι   οτ-
    τη   νῷ
    καὶ θείῳ
     garland
    Ἀρτέμων τὸ
    πηαρις κατ' ἐπ-
    (ιτα)γὴν ἀνέθηκεν
    ἐπὶ τὰ ἴχνη.
    Ἔτους σξθ', μη(νὸς)
    Δαισίου β'.   184-5 A.D.

(See now appendix)

Lydia, exact provenience unknown

86. Terra cotta statuette, with a pedestal shaped like ⌐ ⌐, therefore intended to fit over something. In the possession of Mr. Dikran Serrafian of Beirut, Lebanon.

Dimensions: Height, including pedestal, 67 cm.

    Bibliography: Lane, I, p. 50.

The statuette portrays a female figure, standing draped, the head and both arms broken off. She has on one full-length garment, over which one hip-length garment, belted at waist. The pedestal bears the following inscription:

    Δεσκυλὶς Δεσκύλου
    Μηνὶ Ἀρτεμιδώρου Ἀξί-
    οττα κατέχοντι ὑπὲρ τῶν
    τέκνων εὐχήν.

Environs of *Sebaste Phrygiae* (perhaps *Alia*):
Kırka near Uşak, Turkey (between Uşak and Sıvaslı = *Sebaste*)

87. Stele of white marble with pediment and acroteria, discovered before 1883; in 1932 in Smyrna museum. Now in courtyard of old museum.

Dimensions: Height, ca. 82 cm., width of entablature, 52 cm., width of shaft, 50 cm., thickness of entablature, 18 cm., thickness of shaft, 15 cm.

> Bibliography: Drexler, *op. cit.*, col. 2709; W. A. Ramsay, *JHS*, IV, 1883, p. 417, no. 31; W. M. Ramsay, *Cities and Bishoprics of Phrygia*, Oxford, 1895, p. 609, no. 506; Perdrizet, *op. cit.*, p. 62; Buresch, *Aus Lydien*, p. 131; F. Poland, *Geschichte des Griechischen Vereinswesens*, Leipzig, 1909, p. 53; Robert, *Hellenica*, III, 1946, p. 60, note 3 and Plate III A; Lane, I, p. 22, no. 1.

In the pedimental area there is a bust of a goddess. In the main field, there is a representation of Men riding to the right, with crescent and Phrygian cap. There is a projecting ledge under the horse's feet. Inscription:

a) on entablature under bust:

> Ἀγαθῇ τύχῃ, ἔτους σνδ'.

b) left of Men riding:

> Μηνὶ Ἀσκαη-
> νῷ
> φράτρα Ἡλι-
> οφῶντος
> Ἀντιόχου
> καὶ Πονπε-
> ίου Μάρ-
> κο
> υ

c) right of Men riding:

> ἀνέθηκαν

169-170 A.D.

Alianon katoikia: Kirgil, near Emet, Turkey
(Kirkıl on map)

88. Stele with "corniche" (moulding) discovered by Gen. Callier before 1836.
Dimensions unknown.

> Bibliography: Drexler, *op. cit.*, col. 2709; S. Reinach, *REG*, III, 1890, p. 51, no. 1; Perdrizet, *op. cit.*, pp. 62-3; Lane, I, pp. 22-23, no. 2.

The stone bears the following inscription, of which the first line is on the moulding:

["Ετ]ους σοε' ἀ[····]   190-191 A.D.
Νεικήτας Παρδ-
αλᾶ Μηνὶ θεῷ
εὐχὴν
ὁσίῳ κ(αὶ) δικέῳ.
Ἡ Ἀλιανῶν κα-
τοικία. Σῶζε
τὴν κατοικί-
αν.

Hasarlar (Hasanlar on map), near Emet, Turkey

89. Stone of undetermined type built into the side of a fountain. Found by Munro before 1897.
Dimensions unknown. Letters 1 inch.

> Bibliography: J. A. R. Munro, *JHS*, XVII, 1897, p. 283, no. 48; Buresch, *Aus Lydien*, p. 152; Lane, I, p. 25, no. 21.

The stone bears the following inscription: (Buresch's interpretation)

Κυντιανὴ Κυντιανοῦ
ὑπὲρ τεκέως ἀνέθηκε
τᾷ Ἑκάτᾳ καὶ Μανὶ τὸν
υἱέα τῶ Παιᾶνος.

Synaus: Simav, Turkey

90. Stele of marble, broken on top. Found by Ramsay, 1884, in Simav; by 1889 transported to Kula; by 1904 in bazaar in İstanbul. Now in Warsaw?

Dimensions: Height 37 cm.

>Bibliography: Drexler, *op. cit.*, col. 2701, no. 7; Ramsay, *JHS*, X, 1889, p. 227, no. 25; E. L. Hicks, *Classical Review*, III, 1889, p. 138, no. 19; Buresch, *Reisebericht II*, p. 97; Perdrizet, *op. cit.*, p. 57, no. 3; Buresch, *Aus Lydien*, p. 87 and 197 (as being from Köres); A. E. Kontoleon, *REG*, XIV, 1901, p. 300 (as being from Kireci, 1 1/2 hours from Kula); *Nea Smyrne*, no. 3832; T. Wiegand, *AM*, XXIX, 1904, p. 318, fig. 38; A. Deissmann, *Light from the Ancient East*, 1910 ed., p. 332; Buckler, *ABSA*, XXI, 1914-16, pp. 181-3, no. 6; Deissmann, *Licht vom Osten*[4], 1923, p. 278, note 6 and fig. 58, as in Braunsberg Collection; *Light from the Ancient East*, 1927 ed., p. 328 and fig. 60; Herrmann, *op. cit.*, p. 47, note 183; Lane, I, p. 23, no. 3.

The stone bears a relief field with projecting lower ledge showing Men standing frontally with crescent, cap, etc., holding a staff in his right hand, an indistinct object in his left.

Under the relief it bears the following inscription (rejecting Buckler's interpretation):

>Γαλλικῷ 'Ασκληπιὰς
>κώμης Κερυζέων πα(ι)-
>δίσχη Διογένου
>λύτρον.

Doryleum: Eskişehir, Turkey

91. Small stele with pediment, discovered August-September 1893 in a private house by Radet.

Dimensions unknown.

>Bibliography: Drexler, *op. cit.*, col. 2711; G. Radet, *Nouvelles Archives des Missions Scientifiques et Litteraires*, VI, 1895, p. 573, no. 23; Perdrizet, *op. cit.*, p. 64; Ramsay, *Bearing of Recent Discovery on the Trustworthiness of the New Testament*, London, 1915, p. 184, fig. 4; Lane, I, p. 23, no. 4.

The stele, according to Radet's drawing, has a figure riding right, turned to face the viewer. He is dressed with a hood, and does not have a crescent, and therefore resembles Telesphorus rather than Men.

No. 91

The stone has the following inscription, of which the first line is on the entablature. The following reading, based more on Ramsay than on Radet, is given with all due hesitation:

$$\begin{aligned}&\Pi\alpha\pi\tilde{\alpha}\ \Pi\alpha\pi\tilde{\alpha}\varsigma\\&(\dot{\upsilon}\pi\grave{\varepsilon}\rho)\ \tau\acute{\varepsilon}\kappa\nu\omega\nu\ \sigma\omega\tau\text{-}\\&\eta\rho\acute{\iota}\alpha\varsigma\qquad M\eta\nu\grave{\iota}\\&\varepsilon\grave{\upsilon}\chi\qquad\quad\ \ \mathring{\eta}\nu.\end{aligned}$$

Serea?: Kuyucak, area of Eskişehir, Turkey
(Between Eskişehir and Seyitgazi, as
are next two places)

92. A small altar with palmettes and vertical division in upper moulding. Copied by Sterrett in 1883.
Dimensions unknown.

Bibliography: Ramsay, *Zeitschrift für vergleichende Sprachforschung,*

XXVIII, 1887, p. 394, no. 16; Drexler, *op. cit.*, col. 2711; Ramsay, *Bearing*, p. 187, no. 3; *MAMA* V, (1937) p. 150, no. R7; Lane, I, p. 23, no. 5.

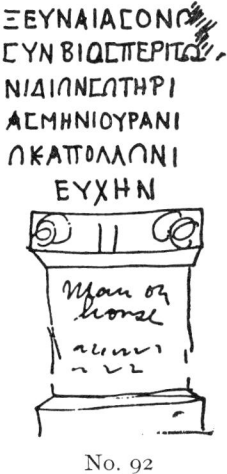

```
ΞΕΥΝΑΙΑΣΟΝΟ
ΣΥΝΒΙΟΣΠΕΡΙΤΩ
ΝΙΔΙΩΝΣΩΤΗΡΙ
ΑΣΜΗΝΙΟΥΡΑΝΙ
ΩΚΑΠΟΛΛΩΝΙ
ΕΥΧΗΝ
```

No. 92

The main field of the altar bears on its right side, an ox-head; on the front, a horseman (Men?). Under the horseman there is the following inscription:

Ξεῦνα ᾽Ιάσονο[ς]
σύνβιος περὶ τῶ-
ν ἰδίων σωτηρί-
ας Μηνὶ Οὐρανί-
ῳ καὶ ᾽Απόλλωνι
εὐχήν.

Oueza ?: Söpüren, area of Eskişehir, Turkey

93. Altar of grayish marble, found in 1931 by C. W. M. Cox, "supporting a shed in Suleyman's house-yard."

Dimensions: Height 83.5 cm., width at top 41 cm., width of shaft 40 cm., thickness of top 40 cm., thickness of shaft 36 cm., height of letters 3 to 3.5 cm.

Bibliography: *MAMA*, V, p. 71, no. 150 and Plate 40; Lane, I, p. 23, no. 5.

The main field bears a relief of a crescent, divided down the middle by a line, a leaf hanging from each end. Under the crescent there is the following inscription:

Οὐεζαεῖται
Μηνὶ Ἰταλ[ι]κῷ
ἐξ ἐπιτα[γ]ῆς.

Aouda?: Avdan, region of Eskişehir, Turkey

94. Small marble cippus, broken. Discovered by Cox in 1931 in home of Ali Effendi.

Dimensions: Height 64 cm., length of shaft 34 cm., circumference of shaft 78 cm., diameter at bottom ca. 29 cm., height of letters 2.25 to 2.75 cm.

> Bibliography: *MAMA*, V, p. 65, no. 132 and Plate 37; Lane, I, p. 23, no. 7.

The stone bears a relief of Men as horseman going right in front of an oversize moon. Under the relief there is an inscription, of which the last line is on the base:

[Τατ]α Τατάδος
[ὑπ]ὲρ παιδίων
[αὐτ]ῆς Μηνὶ Οὐρα-
[νίῳ εὐχ]ήν.

95. Small altar of marble, top buried, broken below and right. Discovered by same person, at same time, in a houseyard in Avdan.

Dimensions: Visible height 51 cm., width at base 27.5 cm., width at shaft 22.5 cm., thickness of base 20 cm., thickness of shaft 17 cm., height of letters 2.0 to 2.5 cm.

> Bibliography: *MAMA*, V, p. 65, no. 133 and Plate 38; Lane, I, p. 23, no. 8.

The stone bears a relief showing the head of Men within a crescent moon. Under it, an inscription, of which the last line is on the base:

Φωτίων κ(αὶ) γυ-
γὴ αὐτοῦ (ὑ)πὲρ

[τ]έκνων Μη-
γὶ Οὐρανίῳ
εὐχή[ν].

Nacoleia: Seyitgazi, Turkey

96. Marble altar buried at bottom. Discovered March-April 1931 by C. E. Stephens, at a fountain beside the Derebenek mosque.

Dimensions: Visible height 76 cm., width at top 43 cm., width of shaft 34 cm., thickness of top 35 cm., thickness of shaft 27 cm., height of letters 2 to 3.5 cm.

Bibliography: *MAMA*, V, p. 100, no. 209 and Plate 48; Lane, I, p. 23, no. 9.

The stone bears a relief of a crescent with appendages at either end and a lug at bottom. Under it is the following inscription, of which the last two lines give the impression that they may have been added later:

Τυχάσ[ι]ος
'Απολλωνίου
Μηνὶ εὐχὴν
Κολιανοκωμή
τη·   -τη[ς]?

97. Limestone altar (?), but if so upper and lower mouldings have been shaved off. Discovered by A. Cameron, 1931, in wall of Derebenek mosque.

Dimensions: Height 80 cm., width 41 cm., thickness 38 cm., height of letters 3 cm.

Bibliography: *MAMA*, V, p. 101, no. 210 and Plate 48; Lane, I, p. 24, no. 10a.

There are no traces of any relief, but there is the following badly worn inscription:

Κωμηνοὶ
Μηνὶ [ε]ὐ-
χὴν
[κα]ὶ Βέγνε[ι].

98. Grey marble altar, discovered by Cameron in 1931 in yard of Sarkır Ahmet. Uncut behind, slightly broken above, with a boss on top surface. Front and sides have palmette acroteria and a vertical bar between them.

Dimensions: Height 95 cm., height of shaft 46 cm., width at top 38 cm., width of shaft 32 cm., width of base 42 cm., thickness of top 36 cm., thickness of shaft 33 cm., thickness of base 42 cm., height of letters 2.4 to 4 cm.

    Bibliography: *MAMA*, V, p. 100, no. 208 and Plate 48; Lane, I, p. 23, no. 10.

The stone bears a relief of a bull's head and under it the following inscription, of which the last line is on the base:

    'Αεζηνο-
    ὶ ἐνχώρι-
    οι Μηνὶ
    Τουιτη-
    [ν]ῷ εὐχήν.

Cottiaeum: Kütahya, Turkey

99. Funerary stele of white marble found (before 1881), presumably in area of Kütahya, although originally reported as being from Thessaloniki. Now in İstanbul Archaeological Museum. Pediment above, lug at bottom.

Dimensions: Height 1.225 m., width at bottom 63 cm., width at top 61 cm., thickness 11.5 cm., lug 9 cm. by 17.5 cm., upper register 36 by 60 cm., lower register 39 by 50.5 cm., height of letters 1.3 cm.

    Bibliography: *S. Reinach, *Catalogue du Musée de Constantinople*, no. 244, p. 36; *A. Joubin, *Sculptures grecques et romaines*, no. 124; Daremberg-Saglio, III, ii, p. 1395, figure 4670; *P. A. Dethier, *Études Archeologiques* (1881), p. 48 and 113ff.; H. Stending in Roschers Lexikon, s.v. *Hekate*, col. 1886; Drexler, *op. cit.*, col. 2768; Mordtmann, *AM* X, 1885, p. 16 (reattribution to Cotiaeum); Perdrizet, *op. cit.*, p. 64ff. and Plate XVI; J. A. R. Munro, *JHS*, XVII, 1897, p. 283-84; H. Usener, *RM*, LVIII, 1903, p. 164; F. Studniczka, *Sächsische Akademie Leipzig, Phil.-Hist. Abhandlungen*, XXII, 4, 1904, p. 133, figure 69; Perdrizet, *RA*, 1904, I, p. 236; E. Michon, *REA*, VIII, 1906, p. 187; O. Gruppe, *Griechische Mythologie und Religionsgeschichte*, II, (1906), p.

1289, note 2; F. von Calice, *Österreichische Jahreshefte*, XI, 1908, Beiblatt, 200; G. Mendel, *BCH*, XXXIII, 1909, p. 286 and 297, sub no. 50; S. Reinach, *Répertoire des Reliefs*, II, p. 174, no. 2; K-P, II Reise, pp. 142-3; Mendel, *Catalogue des Sculptures Grecques, Romaines et Byzantines, Musées Impériaux Ottomans*, Constantinople, 1912-14, III, 314-317, no. 1077; W. H. Buckler et al., *JRS*, XV, 1925, p. 158; M. I. Rostovzeff, *Social and Economic History of the Roman Empire*, 2nd ed., Oxford 1957, p. 256 and Plate XLVI, no. 2; Lane, I, p. 24, no. 11.

The stone bears the following reliefs from top to bottom: Above, make-believe palmette acroteria. In pediment, eagle with outstretched wings facing right, between two roosters.

In upper register, left to right:
Men standing frontally, holding a palm branch in his left hand; a triple Hekate with torches and polos; on the head of the central Hekate a bust of a solar divinity in a sort of crescent; right, a young boy standing naked, in his right hand a double axe, in his left, an indistinct object held out for a dog to eat. Above Men, an open writing tablet; above boy, a crow facing right on a basket, at right above, comb (?) and below, mirror.

Lower register, busts of a man, left, and woman, right, both with their right hands held across their chests. Under them, outside the register, a plow.

On the divider between the two registers, and spilling down to right of lower register, the following inscription:

 Ἄπψιον τὸν ἑαυτῆς σύνβιον Γάειον κατεειέρωσεν σωτίρῃ Ἑ-
 κάτῃ καὶ Ἀπελλᾶς καὶ Γάειος ἐτείμησαν τοὺς ἑαυτῶν γο-
 νῖς μν-
 ήμης
 χάριν.
 Τειμέ-
 ας Μου-
 ρματε-
 ανός.

Area of ancient *Acmoneia*: Hasanköy, Turkey

100. Fragment of stele found by Calder, Birnie, and Watson in April 1933.

Dimensions: Preserved height 32 cm., restored width 42 cm., thickness 6 cm., letters 7.5 cm.

> Bibliography: *MAMA* VI, (1939) p. 92, no. 248 and Pl. 44; Flacelière and Robert, *REG*, LII, 1939, p. 511, no. 407.

Only the top of the stele is preserved, the line of fissure running from upper right to lower left. There is preserved a pediment with floral acroteria at the top, the left corner, and presumably the right corner. In the pedimental area there is a bust of Men, in the left margin between the acroteria a bust of Helios, and in the right margin a bust of Selene. Under the pediment there is preserved the first word of an inscription:

Α··········

Eumeneia Phrygiae: Işıklı, Turkey

101. Stone found in cemetery before 1825, still there in ca. 1884. Dimensions unknown.

> Bibliography: Letronne, *Journal des Savants*, 1825, p. 330 ff.; *CIG*, 3886; Drexler, *op. cit.*, col. 2712; P. Paris, *BCH*, VIII, 1884, p. 237, no. 7; Ramsay, *C and B*, I (1895), p. 246 (cf. also II, p. 355 ff.); Perdrizet, *BCH*, XX, 1896, p. 62; R. Cagnat et al., *Inscriptiones Graecae ad Res Romanas Pertinentes*, Paris, 1911-27, IV, no. 739; Lane, I, p. 24, no. 12; L. Vidman, *op. cit.*, p. 159, no. 311.

The stone bears the following inscription (Ramsay's restoration):

> Ὁ δῆμος ἐτεί[μησεν Αὐρήλιον]
> Μόνιμον Ἀρίστων[ος Ζηνόδο-]
> τον λαμπαδάρχην ἱ[ερέα Διὸς]
> Σωτῆρος καὶ Ἀπόλλ[ωνος καὶ]
> Μηνὸς Ἀσκαηνοῦ [καὶ Μητρὸς]
> θεῶν Ἀνγδίστεω[ς καὶ Ἀγαθοῦ]
> Δαίμονος καὶ Εἴσε[ιδος καὶ Σε-]
> βαστῆς Εἰρήνης, σ[τρατηγὸν]
> τῆς πόλεως τὸ ἕκτον [χρεοφυλα-]
> κήσαντα καὶ ἐγλογισ[τεύσαντα]
> καὶ ἀγορανομήσαντα κ[αὶ εἰρηναρ-]
> χήσαντα καὶ παραφυ[λάξαντα καὶ]
> [γραμ]μ[α]τεύ[σαντα.]

Kaualenon katoikia?: Elmaçık? Turkey
(S. of Uşak, area of ancient *Trajanopolis*)

102. Marble stele with lug known since before 1884. Now in British Museum.
Dimensions: Height 40.5 cm., width 24.5 cm., thickness 7 cm.

> Bibliography: *W. H. Cope, *Journal of the British Archaeological Association*, XL, 1884, pp. 114-5; Drexler, *op. cit.*, col. 2714; Perdrizet, *op. cit.*, p. 63; Robert, *Revue de Philologie*, LXV, 1939, p. 179, note 3 and Plate II, no. 1; Vermaseren, *Vigiliae Christianae*, IV, 1950, p. 151, figure 2; Lane, I, p. 24, no. 13 and Plate III, no. 1; R. A. Higgins, "Recent Acquisitions by the British Museum," *Archaeological Reports*, XIII, 1966-7, pp. 47-48 and fig. 5; Robert, *REG*, LXXXI, 1968, p. 429, no. 71.

The relief shows Men within a sculptured niche, decorated with acroteria, holding a pine-cone in his left hand, a thyrsus (?) in his right, his left foot resting on the head of a prostrate bull. Under the relief there is the following inscription:

> Ἀγαθόπο-
> υς Καουλη-   Μηνὶ
> νῷ εὐχήν.

According to *Sotheby's Sale Catalogue*, 6 July 1964, "the relief is said to have been found at the Royal Mt. Ephraim Hotel, Tunbridge Wells, about 1800, during the reconstruction of the building." Thus either brought there by an early traveler, or actually dedicated there in antiquity.

Ormeleis: Tefenni, Turkey

103. Theater seat found before 1878 in Moslem cemetery.
Dimensions of right outside face: Width 54 cm., thickness 44 cm., height 37 cm.

> Bibliography: Collignon, *BCH*, II, 1878, p. 171-2; J. R. S. Sterrett, *Epigraphical Journey* (Papers of the American School of Classical Studies at Athens, II, 1883-4), p. 94, no. 61; Drexler, *op. cit.*, col. 2716; Berard, *BCH*, XVI, 1892, p. 418; Ramsay, *C and B*, I, p. 304; Perdrizet, *op. cit.*, p. 63; Lane, I, p. 24, no. 14.

The seat bears the following inscription:
On right (Collignon's copy, with supplements)

> Ἀπολλώνι-
> ος Μήνιδος γ´
> Μεσανβριο[ς]
> ἱερατεύων
> Μηνὶ Τολησέ-
> ων εὐχήν.

On back of seat (Sterrett's copy):

261-2 A.D., Cibyratic era

> Ἔτους ϛλσ´, Αὐρ. Φιλι-
> ρος Δημητρίου [Μ]ικ-
> κίου ἱεράσατο.
> Ἔτους ζλσ´, Αὐρ. Πάπης
> Μίδα ἱεράσατο ἐκ τῶν
> ἰδίων θελίως.

On left side (Collignon's copy):

> ΙΙ Α
>   Ρ ΙΙ ΙΙ ΤΟ Μοδίωνο[ς]
> ΔΟ. Ν ὑπάρχοντος
> ΠΥΤΟΕΣ κατὰ τό
> τε ἱερίον καὶ ΘΕΔ
>   ΟΣ

Olbasa: Belenli, Turkey, near Tefenni

104. Rectangular altar of white marble, known since before 1923. Formerly in "caserna nuova" in Burdur, now in Antalya Museum.

Dimensions: Height 54 cm., width 29 cm., thickness 22 cm., height of letters 2.5 cm. (Metzger gives further details).

> Bibliography: B. Pace, *Annuario*, VI-VII, 1923-4, pp. 448-9, no. 167; *SEG*, VI, 1932, p. 103, no. 607; XVII, 1960, p. 149, no. 549; H. Metzger, *Catalogue des monuments votifs du Musée d'Adalia*, Paris, 1952, p. 48, no. 22 and Plate XI; Bean, *Belleten*, XXII, 1958, p. 69, no. 85; Lane, I, p. 43-4, no. 4.

ASIA MINOR 69

The stone bears a relief of Men riding to the right, crescent at shoulders, turned to face viewer with deliberately featureless face. In his right hand he holds a pine-cone. The horse also has face to viewer. The following inscription is arranged with the last two lines on the base, the rest around the figure of Men:

Αὐρ. 'Αντίοχος
Νέω   νος
[Σ]κρ   αίου
Μη-
νὶ
ἐπηκόῳ εὐ-
χήν.

Appola?: Çoğu (Kaçubi) Turkey
(Between Bolvadin and Emirdağ)

105. Round pillar of bluish limestone, broken below. Found in 1908 by W. M. Calder, beside a mosque.
Dimensions: Height 79 cm., circumference 1.23 m., height of letters 2 to 2.5 cm.

  Bibliography: W. M. Calder, *Klio*, X, 1910, p. 241, no. 14; *MAMA*, I, (1928) p. 231, no. 436; Lane, I, p. 24, no. 15.

The stone bears the following inscription, beginning 63 cm. from the top:

Ὑπὲρ δήμου 'Αππολη-
νῶν σωτηρίας Μηνὶ
'Ασκαηνῷ εὐχὴν Δη-
[μοσθέν]ης Διο[τείμου].

Vicinity of *Laodiceia Combusta:* Hacılar, Turkey
(Hacısofrazlar on map, S. of Kadınhani)

106. Limestone lion with head broken off, found in 1928.
Dimensions: Height 95 cm., width 34 cm., thickness 71 cm., height of letters 2.25 to 2.75 cm.

```
ΡΩΝΙΟC
ΕΥCΑΠΠΑC ΥΕ
    ΜΗΙ ΑCΚΑΗΝΩ
         Ν
```

No. 106

Bibliography: *MAMA*, VII, (1956) p. 1, no. 4 and p. 125; Lane, I, p. 25, no. 16.

On the front of the base, broken on left, is the following inscription:

[Πετ]ρώνιος
[····]ευς ῎Αππας ὑε[ι-]
[ὸς αὐτοῦ Μ]ηνὶ ᾿Ασκαηνῷ
[εὐχ]ήν.

Selmea: Gözören, Turkey (Kozviran on map)

107. Marble (?) altar, with sides trimmed off. Discovered in 1898 in cemetery by J. W. Crowfoot and J. G. C. Anderson.

Dimensions: Height 1.44 m., width 34 cm., thickness 51 cm., height of letters 2.5 to 3 cm.

Bibliography: J. G. C. Anderson, *JHS*, XIX, 1899, p. 299, no. 220; *MAMA*, VII, p. 52, no. 243 and Plate XV; Lane, I, p. 25, no. 17.

The main field of the altar bears a relief of Men riding right, facing viewer, with spear in right hand, and crescent behind neck. On back, grapes hanging from a stem with two leaves. Under the main relief, the following inscription:

Αὐρ. Παπᾶς Γαίου
κὲ Γάιος Παπᾶς ὁ
υἱὸς αὐτοῦ ὑπὲ[ρ]
[τ]ῆς ἑαυτῶν σω[τη-]
[ρί]ας Μηνὶ Σελμεην[ῷ]
εὐχήν.

108. Altar (marble?) discovered by Crowfoot and Anderson in 1898 in cemetery at Gözören.

Dimensions: Height 1.48 m., width at top 61 cm., width of shaft 56 cm., width of base 59 cm., thickness 55 cm., height of letters 2.5 to 3 cm.

> Bibliography: Anderson, *op. cit.*, p. 299, no. 221; *MAMA*, VII, p. 52, no. 244 and Pl. 15; Lane, I, p. 25, no. 18.

The main field shows Men on pedestal, ox-head by left foot, defaced object in right hand, left hand raised with elbow on pillar (?). On left side, ox-head. On right side, grapes and leaves as before. Above the main relief, the following inscription:

[ὁ δῆ]μος Σελμηνῶν
[Μ]ηνὶ εὐχήν.

109. Altar (marble?) broken left and below. Found in 1928 (?) by W. M. Calder's party.

Dimensions: Height .54 m., width .35 m., thickness .35 m., height of letters 1.25 to 1.5 cm.

> Bibliography: *MAMA*, VII, p. 52, no. 245 and p. 133; Lane, I, p. 25, no. 19.

No. 109

The altar has a representation of "horns," then a moulding with a vegetative decoration, then a relief field. In the field, Men standing with left arm raised. Inscription with first three lines between horns, 4th on moulding:

$$[\cdots\cdots]\alpha\iota o[\varsigma]$$
$$[M\eta\nu\grave{\iota}\ \Sigma\epsilon]\lambda\mu\eta\nu\tilde{\omega}$$
$$[\epsilon\grave{\upsilon}]\chi\acute{\eta}\nu$$
$$\alpha\rho\sigma\upsilon\qquad\iota o$$

Area of *Vetissus?*: Yağcı Oğlu, Turkey
(Near Sülüklü)

110. Altar, only one side of which is visible. Found by Calder and Ramsay in 1912 (?).

Dimensions: Height .63 m., width .58 m., height of letters .02 to .03 m.

> Bibliography: W. M. Calder, *Klio*, XXIV, 1930, p. 62; *SEG*, VI, (1932), p. 15, no. 78; *MAMA*, VII, p. 76, no. 311 and p. 137; Lane, II, p. 44, Addenda, no. 1.

No. 110

The altar bears a relief of a bull's head within a wreath. The following inscription is on the upper moulding with the last word between the bull's horns:

$$[\Delta\iota]o\gamma\acute{\epsilon}\nu\eta\varsigma\ {}^{\backprime}E\rho\mu\acute{\epsilon}\rho\omega\tau o\varsigma\ \grave{\upsilon}\pi\grave{\epsilon}[\rho]$$
$$\dot{\epsilon}\alpha\upsilon\tau o\tilde{\upsilon}\ \varkappa\alpha\grave{\iota}\ \tau\acute{\epsilon}\varkappa\nu\omega\nu\ M\eta\nu\grave{\iota}$$
$$\epsilon\grave{\upsilon}\chi\acute{\eta}\nu.$$

(Büyük) Beşkavak, Turkey

111. Fragment (of marble) broken all around. Found by W. M. Calder's party in 1928.

Dimensions: Height 51 cm., width 34 cm., thickness 9 cm., height of letters 2.25 cm.

    Bibliography: *MAMA*, VII, p. 105, no. 486 and Pl. 27; Lane, I, p. 25, no. 20.

The stone bears the following inscription:

                                  89-90 A.D., Galatian era.

        Λούκιος Σέργι[ος]
        Κόρινθος Μην[ὶ···]
        πυκηνῷ εὐχὴν τό[ν]
        τε ναὸν ἐκ τῶν ἰδίων
        ἐποίησεν, ἔτους
           ριδ'.

Julia Ipsus [1]: Çay, Turkey

112. Small stele with representation of pediment, acroteria, etc. Broken at bottom. Reportedly found in area of Julia-Ipsus, now in museum at Afyon Karahissar.

Dimensions unavailable; ca. 8 inches tall.

    Bibliography: Lane, I, p. 26, no. 23, Plate IV, no. 1.

The main field shows Men riding right, holding indistinct object in right hand, his gaze directed toward the viewer and slightly down. Instead of the usual Phrygian cap, he seems to wear a hood, and he also has on a military cuirass (?). If there was originally an inscription, it is now missing. (Fuller publication of this and the following four items is reserved by members of the museum staff.)

113. Small stele with pediment and acroteria. Preserved entire.

---

[1] For the most recent discussion of the topography of this area, and the fact that Ipsus should probably be dissociated from Julia, see M. H. Ballance, *AS*, XIX, 1969, pp. 143-146.

Found reportedly in area of Julia-Ipsus, now in museum of Afyon Karahissar.

Dimensions unavailable; ca. 1 foot tall.

Bibliography: Lane, I, p. 26, no. 24, Plate IV, no. 2.

The pedimental area has the representation of a crescent in relief. In the main area of the stele there is the following inscription:

Πυλάδης
Διομᾶ
Μηνὶ
εὐχήν.

114. Small stele with pediment and acroteria. Found reportedly in area of Julia-Ipsus, now in museum of Afyon Karahissar.

Dimensions: unavailable; ca. 6 inches tall.

Bibliography: Lane, I, p. 26, no. 25, Plate IV, no. 3.

The stone bears a representation of a crescent moon in the main field, under which there is the following inscription:

Ἄππας Ἀλεξάνδρο-
υ Μηνὶ εὐχήν.

115. Small stele broken at top. Found reportedly in area of Julia-Ipsus, now in museum of Afyon Karahissar.

Dimensions unavailable; ca. 6 inches tall.

Bibliography: Lane, I, p. 26-27, no. 26.

The stone bears in the main field a relief of a crescent moon, with appendages at either end and a ball in the middle. Around and below the relief the following inscription is arranged:

Πα   πᾶς
Μη   νὶ
Ξευναγονη-
νῷ εὐχήν.

116. Terracotta statuette, broken at bottom, missing head, parts of both arms, and right half of crescent. Found reportedly in area of Julia-Ipsus, now in Afyon Museum.

Dimensions unavailable; ca. 4 inches tall.

Bibliography: Lane, I, p. 27, no. 27, Plate VI, no. 3.

Men wears a chiton tied at the waist and a long cloak. The left hand was raised, as if to hold a staff, and the right hand, outstretched, must have held a pine-cone or similar attribute.

117. A statue of Men on white marble, found in 1964 or 1965 at Çavdarlitepe-Sülümenli. Now in Afyon Museum. Ca. 1 foot high.

Men (his head broken off) is shown standing with a column under his left elbow, a bull's head under his left foot. Full publication is reserved by Prof. Nezih Fıratlı of İstanbul.

Aphrodisias: Geyre, Turkey

118. Marble block, cut above, found in city wall, still *in situ*. First copied by Dr. Sherard in 1705. "Rampart between e. angle and e. door."

Dimensions: Height 1.005 m., width .74 m., thickness .34 m., height of letters, lines 1-13, 2.5 to 3.5 cm.
    lines 14-17, 2.25 to 2.75 cm.

Bibliography: *CIG*, II, p. 523, no. 2796; Le Bas-Waddington, III, p. 393, no. 1601 b.; Drexler, *op. cit.*, col. 2698; O. Liermann, *Analecta epigraphica et agonistica*, (Dissertationes Philologicae Halenses, X, 1889), pp. 17-19, no. III; Reinach, *REG*, XIX, 1906, p. 147, no. 79; L. Robert, *Études Anatoliennes*, Paris, 1937, p. 313, note 2; *MAMA*, VIII, (1962) p. 73, no. 406; Lane, I, p. 27, no. 1; Robert, *Hellenica*, XIII, 1965, p. 183 and 285.

The stone bears the following inscription:

[· · · · · · · · · · · ·εὐν]οίᾳ καὶ κ[οι-]
νῶς πρὸς πάντας καὶ ἰδίᾳ πρ[ὸς]
ἕκαστον φιλανθρώπως καὶ πλείσ-
τας ἐγγύας ὑπὲρ πολλῶν ἐκτε[ί-]
σαντα καὶ ἱερεύσαντα πρὸ πό-
λεως τῆς Ἑκάτης ὁσίως καὶ
εὐσεβῶς. Συνεχωρήθη αὐτῷ
καὶ ἐνταφὴν ἐν τῷ γυμνασίῳ,
δίδοσθαι δὲ αὐτῷ καὶ ἀπὸ

τῶν δημοσίᾳ θυομένων γέρα,
ἐξεῖναι δὲ αὐτῷ καὶ τοὺς στε-
φάνους φορεῖν οἷς ἐστεφάνω-
ται ὅταν βούληται.
Καλλικράτης Μολοσσοῦ ἱερεὺς
Μηνὸς Ἀσκαινοῦ καὶ Ἑρμοῦ Ἀγοραίου
τὰς τῶν προπατόρων τιμὰς
ἐπισκευάσας ἀποκατέστησεν.

119. Moulded marble block in city wall. Found by Calder in 1934. Dimensions: Height .27 m., width ca. 1.33 m., visible thickness 6.9 cm., height of letters 2.25 to 3 cm.

Bibliography: *MAMA*, VIII, p. 94, no. 445; Lane, I, p. 27, no. 2; Robert, *Hellenica*, XIII, p. 128, note 2.

The stone bears the following inscription:

Ἡρακλεῖ καὶ τῷ [δή]μ[ῳ]   [τ]ὴν [τρά]πεζαν
Καλλικράτης Μολο[σσοῦ ἱε]ρε[ὺς] Μηνὸς
Ἀ[σκ]αινοῦ καὶ Ἑρμοῦ [Ἀγο]ραίου

120. Two joining marble fragments in a wall near the stadium. Found by Calder in 1934.

Dimensions: a) height 47 cm.   b) height 25 cm.
             width 27 cm.   width 13 cm.
             letters 2 to 2.5 cm.

Bibliography: *MAMA*, VIII, p. 94, no. 446 and Pl. 36; Lane, I, p. 27, no. 3; Robert, *Hellenica*, XIII, p. 128-9.

The stone bears the following inscription (Robert's restoration of first two lines):

Νίκη πά[ρ]ειμ[ι]
Καίσαρ[ι] ἀεί.
Θεοῖς Σεβαστο[ῖς καὶ τῶι]
δήμωι τὴν Νίκη[ν καὶ τὸν]
[λ]έοντα   Καλ[λικράτης]
[Μ]ολοσσοῦ ἱε[ρεὺς Μηνὸς Ἀσ-]
καινοῦ καὶ Ἑρ[μοῦ Ἀγοραίου, τὰ]
[προ]γονικὰ ἀν[αθήματα πάντα]
[ἐπ]ισκευάσας [ἀποκατέστησεν].

Burdur, Turkey

121. An altar now in the Antalya museum (since 1946 at least), said to have come from Burdur.

Dimensions: Height 86.5 cm., width 42 cm., thickness 38 cm.

> Bibliography: L. Robert, *Hellenica*, IX, 1950, p. 39ff. and Plates VI, VII, and VIII; *REG*, LXIV, 1951, p. 191, no. 217; W. Klaffenbach, *Gnomon*, XXIII, 1951, p. 390; Robert, *REG*, LXV, 1952, p. 176, no. 155; George Bean, *JHS*, LXXII, 1952, p. 118; Robert, *REG*, LXVI, 1953, p. 178, no. 198; Bean, *Belleten*, XXII, 1958, p. 69-70, no. 86; Robert, *REG*, LXXII, 1959, p. 254, no. 442; *SEG*, XVII, 1960, p. 148, no. 545; Lane, I, p. 43, no. 3.

The stone bears an inscription on one face and reliefs on three faces.

Taking the inscribed face as front, the right face bears a relief of a goddess sitting in a throne with a high, wide back. She wears a polos from the top of which fall long ornaments onto her shoulders. In her left hand she holds a scepter ending in a pine-cone like object.

On the left face: Hermes, cloak behind his shoulders, petasus on (damaged) head, left hand holding caduceus, right hand purse (?). On face opposite main inscription, Men on horseback going right at a gallop, head turned toward spectator. Deliberately faceless. Right hand holds bridle. Cloak floats in the wind, attached at right shoulder. He wears a sharp-pointed headdress, and has a crescent just visible at the neck. On the projecting ledge under the figure of Men there is the following inscription:

['Αρτέ]μων Αἰλίο[υ] Μυ[··············]
ἠργάσετο

The main face of the altar bears the following inscription (Bean's restoration):

['Ρό]δων Νεωγ[ος] Σώσου, παρ[ε]-
δρος τοῦ Μηνὸς κλεί-
νας δύο σὺν καταρτισμῷ
καὶ τραπέζας δύο
[ἀ]νακλιτήρια τέσσερα
[σὺν καὶ τῷ] πε[ρ]ιβόλῳ κα[ὶ]

[. . . . .]τὴν μέσην κα[ὶ]
[θυ]ρίδα κανκελλωτὴν
τὴν ἐποῦσα τῷ ταμί[ῳ]
καὶ κῆπον σὺν τῷ πεπ[η-]
γμένῳ ξυλικῷ καὶ θησαυ-
[ρὸν . . . .]ον καὶ ✶ ἐξ ἰς ξυ-
λοθ[ήκ]ην καὶ τοὺς βωμοὺς
[τ]οῦ ε[ἰργ]μοῦ, ὑφ' ἓν ✶ τ', ἐκ
[τῶν ἰδίων ἀ]νέθηκεν.

ΜΗΝΟΓΑC
ΤΡΟΦΙΜΟ
ΜΗΝΙΕΥ
ΧΗΝ

No. 122

122. Cippus built into wall of church of St. George in Burdur as of 1879.

ASIA MINOR

Dimensions: Height 30 cm., width 15 cm.

> Bibliography: M. Collignon, *BCH*, III, 1879, p. 334, no. 2; Drexler, *op. cit.*, col. 2725; Perdrizet, *op. cit.*, p. 63 and figure 2; Lane, I, p. 45, no. 9.

The stone bears a relief of Men riding right, facing the viewer. The right hand was holding out some object now defaced. Under the ledge that the horse stands on, there is the following inscription:

>> Μηνογᾶς
>> Τροφίμο[υ]
>> Μηνὶ εὐ-
>> χήν.

123. Anepigraphical relief of marble reportedly from area of Burdur. Now in Museum of Fine Arts, Boston.

Dimensions: Height 31.7 cm., width 37.8 cm., thickness 9.9 cm. bottom, 4.8 cm. top.

> Bibliography: Lane, I, p. 45, no. 13 and frontispiece.

The relief with a moulding surrounding it is of relatively good workmanship and shows Men riding a horse right. The horse has his left forefoot on a bucranium. Men is portrayed as quite youthful, with the usual flying cloak, Phrygian cap, chiton, and trousers, crescent at shoulders. With his left hand he holds the horse's bridle, and with his right he holds a pine-cone.

Askeriye, 5 km. N.E. of Burdur, Turkey

124. An altar of white marble, in 1959 beside fountain by coffeehouse, said to have been brought from Tekke, just outside the village to the south.

Dimensions: Height 92 cm., width 39 cm., thickness 29 cm.

> Bibliography: Bean, AS, IX, 1959, p. 73, no. 12 and Plate XIV; L. Robert, *REG*, LXXIV, 1961, p. 241, no. 728; *SEG*, XIX, 1963, p. 235, no. 745; Lane, I, p. 44, no. 6.

The main face of the altar bears a relief of Men on horseback going right. Again the face seems deliberately unclear but the crescent is distinguishable. There were reliefs on left and right, but they were almost entirely chiseled away for the stone to be re-used. That on right perhaps depicted some kind of animal. On the moulding above the main relief is the following inscription:

[Μη]νὶ ἐπηκόῳ εὐχή[ν].

Sagalassus (?): Ağlasun, Turkey

125. Small votive altar known since before 1954, now in museum at Burdur. Said to be from Ağlasun, but cf. Robert, *REG*, LXIX, 1956, p. 175.
Dimensions: Height 34 cm.

> Bibliography: G. E. Bean, *Belleten*, XVIII, 1954, pp. 476-7 and 497-99, no. 8; figures 10-12; Robert, *REG*, LXIX, 1956, pp. 174ff., no. 319; *SEG*, XIV, 1957, p. 187, no. 800; Lane, I, p. 44, no. 5.

The stone bears the following three reliefs: on front, a god riding right with cloak flying in the wind, no apparent crescent. On right side, a winged caduceus. On left side, an object which resembles a palm tree supporting a large pine-cone. The front side also bears the following inscription, of which the first three lines are on the upper moulding, the last two on the relief field (Bean's conjectural restoration):

['Ο δεῖνα Τρο-]
[φί]μου Ζω[τι-]
[κοῦ] Μην[ὶ]
ἐπηκόῳ εὐ-
χή   ν.

Macropedium: Akören, Turkey
S. of W. end of lake of Burdur

126. Altar with mouldings and acroteria. Formerly built into fountain. Two sides known since 1888, two others only completely since 1959. Now (1959) outside house of Osman Karakuzu.
Dimensions: Height 1.19 m., width 44 cm., thickness 44 cm.

Bibliography: Ramsay, *AJA*, IV, 1888, p. 19; *C and B*, I, p. 308, no. 120; *The Social Basis of Roman Power in Asia Minor*, Aberdeen, 1941, p. 17, no. 6; Bean, *AS*, IX, 1959, p. 103, no. 64; Robert, *REG*, LXXIV, 1961, p. 242, no. 738; *SEG*, XIX, p. 249, no. 796; Lane, I, p. 44, no. 7.

All four sides of the altar bear inscriptions and reliefs:
Front: relief, perhaps a figure seated in a chariot facing right, a team of horses in front of him. Inscription:

On moulding:
>Ἔτους ΒΡΡΝ.

Above relief:
>καὶ τῷ δήμῳ τῷ Μα-
>κροπεδειτῶν

Below relief:
>Τρωίλος Ὠφελίωνος
>Ὀσάει καὶ Τάτεις Ἀγα-
>θείνου ἡ γυνὴ αὐτοῦ
>καὶ Τρωίλος δὶς καὶ Ἀ-
>γαθεῖνος Ὀσάει τὰ τέ-
>κνα αὐτῶν ἐκ τῶν ἰδί-

On the lower moulding:
>ων κατασκευάσαντες

Left side, reliefs from top to bottom: a horseman, a scorpion?, a garland with hanging grapes. Underneath, the inscription:

>Χρυσοκό   μην Παιᾶνα
>ον ἠύκομο   ς τέκε Λητώ,
>Ἥλιον φαέθοντα λελου-
>[μ]ένον Ὠκεανοῖο, εἴλε-
>ον ἀνθρώποισιν οἳ ἐν-
>θάδε ναιετάουσιν ❦

On bottom moulding:
>Σέλευκος Κιβυρά[της]
>ἐποίει

Back, relief of Zeus on throne, scepter in right hand; on left, long-robed female figure; below, garland and hanging bunch of grapes.

Under the relief the following inscription:

ὑψίθρον   ον βασιλῆ-
α καὶ Ἥρην χρυσεόμι-
τρον, Ἑρ   μῆν τε κλυτ[ό]-
μητιν ἀπαγγέλλαντα [βρο-]
τοῖσι ὅσσα Ζεὺς φρονέει
ἠδὲ ἀθάνατοι θεο[ὶ ἄ]λλοι,

Right side: Relief of horseman, but presence or absence of crescent not determinable. Below, garland with hanging grapes. Inscription: Above the relief:

Μῆνα φιλάνθρωπον πο-
λυάρητον βασιλῆα,

Below the relief:

γράψας ὧδε   ἀνέθηκε
σὺν εὐχωλῇ   σι ἀγανῇσι
Τρωίλος Ὠφελίωνος, ἑῇ
σὺν κεδνῇ ἀκοίτει, ἀνδρά-
σιν ἠδὲ γυναιξὶ σαόφροσιν
εἵλεον αἰεί. ෴

Plouristra?, area of ancient *Tymandos*:
Pise, Başköy on map, Turkey

127. Limestone altar with acroteria and mouldings above and below, discovered by W. H. Buckler's party in the spring of 1930 in the house of Ali Hoca.

Dimensions: Height 81 cm., width 43 to 48 cm., thickness 40 to 43 cm., height of letters 2 to 2.5 cm.

Bibliography: *MAMA*, IV, (1933) p. 83-84, no. 230 and Pl. 49; Lane, I, p. 45, no. 10.

The shaft bears a relief of a male figure standing with spear or staff in right hand, roundish object in left. He wears a tunic girt at waist. The face is featureless. There is a crescent at neck (?). The same side bears the following inscription, of which the first line is between the acroteria, nos. 2 and 3 on the moulding, no. 4 above the relief:

Οἱ περὶ Αὐρ.
Ἀρτέμωνα Ἑρμοκλ[έ-]
ους φράτρα Μηνὶ
Πλουριστρέων εὐχήν.

Aziziye, Turkey
To S. of ancient sites of *Hadriani* and *Moatra*

128. An altar of white marble with acroteria and round superstructure. In 1959 outside house of Arif Sertaç.
Dimensions: Height 93 cm., width 34 cm., thickness 34 cm.

Bibliography: Bean, *AS*, IX, 1959, p. 111, no. 81 and Pl. XX; Robert, *REG*, LXXIV, 1961, p. 243, no. 741; *SEG*, XIX, p. 254, no. 814; Lane, I, pp. 44-45, no. 8.

The stone bears the following relief on the front: Men on horseback to right, face featureless, long crescent at shoulders. On right, a wreath with ribbons; on left, partly obscured, a "bunch of grapes (?) with an appendage below resembling a leg and foot." On back, an ear of grain. On the main face, over the figure of Men, the following inscription:

[· · · · ·]ας δὶς Μουσαίο[υ]
τὸν βωμὸν ἐκ τῶν
[ἰ]δίων Μηνὶ εὐχήν.

Andeda: Andya or Yavuz, Turkey

129. A small round altar supporting a post of the mosque at Belen, 15 minutes (by foot?) from Yavuz. Largely buried when seen by Bean in 1959, and most of copy made by a villager.
Dimensions unavailable.

Bibliography: Bean, *AS*, X, 1960, p. 65, no. 115; Robert, *REG*, LXXIV, 1961, p. 244, no. 748; *SEG*, XIX, p. 263, no. 847; Lane, I, p. 45, no. 11.

The stone bears no relief, but the following inscription:

Κοίντος
Νουμέρι-
ος ἱερεὺς
Μηνὸς Ο[ὐ-]
ρανίου κα-
τὰ χρημα-
τισμὸν ἀνέ-
θηκε θεῷ
ὑψίστῳ.

Apollonia Pisidiae: near Uluborlu, Turkey

130. Stone in the wall of the Greek church in the citadel, discovered by C. Wilson, known since 1883.
Dimensions unavailable.

Bibliography: Ramsay, *JHS*, IV, 1883, p. 417, no. 32; Drexler, *op. cit.*, col. 2723; Perdrizet, *op. cit.*, p. 69; H. Rott, *Kleinasiatische Denkmäler aus Pisidien, Pamphylien, Kilikien, und Lykien* (Studien über christliche Denkmäler, V-VI, Leipzig, 1908), p. 348, no. 1; Robert, *Hellenica*, VI, 1948, p. 34; Lane, I, p. 45, no. 12.

The stone apparently bears a relief of Men riding and the inscription:

"Ορος ἱερὸς καὶ ἄσυ-
λος θεοῦ ἐπιφανοῦ[ς]
Μηνὸς 'Ασκ[α]ινοῦ.

Anaboura: Ördekçi, near Şarkıkaraağaç, Turkey

131. A "handsome monument," found by Calder before 1932. Now in Karaağaç? Two curved entablature blocks, once contiguous.
Dimensions: Height 53 cm., thickness at top 46 cm., at base 35 cm., external width above 1.66, internal width above 1.37, external width below 1.58m.

Bibliography: Calder, *AJA*, XXXVI, 1932, p. 454, no. 7; *MAMA* VIII, p. 62-63, no. 351 and Plate 16; Lane, I, p. 42-43, no. 1a.

The text as printed by the MAMA reads as follows:

['Αναβουρέων ὁ δῆμος ···]ν Τουλιανδου ἱερέα ἐξ ἱερέων Μηνὸς 'Ασκαηνοῦ τὸν ἑα[υ]τῶν [φι]λόπατριν κ[αὶ εὐεργέτην.]

The photograph shows one block with the inscription ending at the word Μηνὸς. Above the band bearing the inscription is a decoration of acanthus leaves (?).

The next five monuments form a closed group, that of the so-called dice-oracles. Since Men is not involved here in any way that has cult significance, I have seen fit to omit all portions of the accompanying inscriptions except the epigram in which Men's name is mentioned.

132. Inscription carved on the concave side of a large block, discovered by Sterrett in 1885.
Dimensions: Length 1.36 m., height 1.24 m.

> Bibliography: Sterrett, *Wolfe Expedition* (Papers of American School of Classical Studies in Athens, III, 1884-5), p. 206-214, no. 339-342; Drexler, *op. cit.*, col. 2720; G. Kaibel, *Hermes*, XXIII, 1888, p. 532ff.; Perdrizet, *op. cit.*, p. 68, no. 2; F. Heinevetter, *Würfel- und Buchstabenorakel in Griechenland und Kleinasien*, Breslau, 1912, no. 3; Lane, I, p. 42, no. 1.

The epigram regarding Men on this oracle runs as follows:

κε' δςςςγ'   Μηνὸς Φωσφόρου
Τέσσαρα δ' εἰς πείπτων, τρεῖς δ' ἐξεῖται, τρί' ὁ πέμπτος
θάρσε, καιρὸν ἔχεις, πράξεις δ' ἃ θέλεις, ἐπιτεύξῃ
εἰς ὁδὸν ὁρμηθῆναι. Ἔχει καρπόν τιν' ὁ μόχθος,
ἔργον δ' ἐνχειρεῖν ἀγαθὸν καὶ ἀγῶνα δίκην τε.

Termessus: Güllük, Turkey

133. Square basis, inscribed on three sides, back rough. On top, remains of an area for rolling dice. Found lying on ground, before 1890, near wall west of temple no. 3, broken into several fragments.

Dimensions: Height 1.87 m., breadth 60 cm., thickness 52 cm., height of letters 1 to 3 cm.

Bibliography: Karl Lanckoronski, *Städte Pamphyliens und Pisidiens*, Vienna, 1890-92, II, pp. 220-223, no. 180; R. Heberdey, *Termessis he Studien*, Vienna Akad., Denkschriften, Phil.-Hist. Klasse, LXIX, 3, 1929, p. 131; *Wiener Studien*, L, 1932, p. 82ff.; *TAM*, III, i, (1941) no. 34, pp. 22-33.

No. 133

The epigram attributed to Men on this dice-oracle is essentially the same as that given to the mother of the gods on the preceding, and vice versa:

ϛϛϛϛα′ κε′   Μηνὸς Φωσφόρου
Τέσσαρες ἐξεῖται, πέμπτος χεῖος, τάδε φράζει,

ὡς ἄρνας κατέχουσι λύκοι κρατεροί τε λέοντες
βοῦς ἕλικας, πάντων τούτων καὶ σὺ κρατήσεις
καὶ πάντ' ἔσται σοι, ὅσ' ἐπερωτᾷς, σὺν Διὸς Ἑρμῇ.

İncik—area of Antalya *(Attaleia)*, Turkey

134. Discovered early in June 1911 by E. S. G. Robinson and H. A. Ormerod beside deserted village of İncik, some six hours (on foot) to the N.E. of Antalya, towards the N.W. corner of site, near the ruins of an apsidal building (Byzantine church). Stone damaged severely within the same summer. A pillar, on which a capital originally sat.

Dimensions: Height 93 cm., width 63 cm., thickness 54 cm., (capital another 40 cm. high); letters mostly 1.6 cm.

Bibliography: Ormerod, *JHS*, XXXII, 1912, pp. 270-276.

The epigram attributed to Men here is virtually the same as on no. 132, and obviously copied from the same original:

δϛϛϛγ'   κε'   [Μ]ηνὸς Φωσφόρου
τέσσαρα εἷς πείπτων, [τρε]ῖς δ' ἐξεῖται, κ[αὶ τ]ρεῖος ὁ πένπτος,
θάρσει, καιρὸν ἔχεις, πράξεις ἃ θέλεις, καιροῦ ἐπιτε[ύ]ξῃ
εἰς ὁδὸν ὁρμηθ[ῆ]ναι, ἔχει καρ(π)όν τ[ιν' ὁ] μόχθος
ἔργον δ' ἐνχειρεῖ[ν] ἀγαθὸν καὶ ἀγῶνα δίκην τε.

Saracık (Saraycık on map) in east *Lycia* ancient name unknown

135. Stone found some time prior to 1944, on the ground, in the south part of the "arx."

Dimensions: Height 1.65 m., width 66 cm., thickness 63 cm.

It also has an upper "crepido" 30 cm. high and 86 cm. both wide and thick. Letters are 1.5 cm., except in lines 1-3, where they are 2.5 cm.

Bibliography: *TAM*, II, iii, (1944) 1222.

This stone bears essentially the same inscription regarding Men, very badly worn:

δςςςγ'   κε'   Μηνὸς Φωσφόρου
[Τ]εσσαρα δ' εἴ(ς) πείπτων, τρεῖς δὲ ἐξῖται, τρί' ὁ πέμπτος,
[θά]ρσει, καιρὸν ἔχεις, πράξεις ἃ θέ[λ]εις, καιρ[οῦ τ]ε ἐπιτεύ[ξῃ]
εἰς ὁδὸν [ὁ]ρμηθῆναι, ἔχει καιρόν τινα ὁ μόχθος,
ἔργον τ' ἐ[γχ]ιρεῖν ἀγ[α]θὸν καὶ ἀγῶν(α) δίκην τε.

Attaleia Pamphyliae: Antalya, Turkey

136. Stone built into a wall in a street not far from harbor (as of 1910). Known since before 1850.
Dimensions: unavailable.

> Bibliography: H. Barth, *RM*, VII, 1850, p. 251; Hirschfeld, *Akademie der Wissenschaften, Berichte*, Berlin, 1875, p. 716; *Hermes*, X, 1876, 19 ff.; G. Kaibel, *Epigrammata Graeca ex Lapidibus Conlecta*, Berlin, 1878, no. 1038; Drexler, *op. cit.*, col. 2720; A. M. Woodward, *JHS*, XXX, 1910, pp. 260-62; Heinevetter, *op. cit.*, no. 1.

Essentially the same epigram is ascribed to Men here also:

δςςςγ'   κε'   Μηνὸς Φωσφόρου
[θά]ρσι, καιρὸν ἔχις, πράξις ὃ θέλις, καιροῦ δ'ἐπιτε[ύξῃ]
[ἰς ὁ]δὸν ὁρμηθῆνε, ἔχις καιρόν τιν' ὁ μόχθος
[ἔρ]γον τ' ἐνχειρῖν ἀγαθὸν καὶ ἀγῶανα δίκ[ην τε].

137. A bronze statuette since 1897 in the Rijksmuseum van Oudheden, Leiden. Said to be from Antalya.
Dimensions: Height 14 cm.

> Bibliography: *Leiden Museum Annual Report*, 1896-7, pp. 5-6; U. Hiesinger, *HSCP*, LXXI, 1966, pp. 306-7 and Plate III; Lane, II, p. 46, no. 10.

Men is shown standing turned to left. The garb is the conventional, perhaps a little longer, as on the Antiochene coin-type. The left foot rests on a bucranium. The right hand held a staff; the left hand holds a pine-cone.

Uncertain provenience

138. Bronze statuette of Men acquired by Fogg Art Museum, Harvard University in 1964.

Dimensions: Height 13.5 cm.

> Bibliography: Hiesinger, *op. cit.*, pp. 303-306, Plate I-II; Lane, II, p. 46, no. 9.

Men stands frontally, a pine-cone extended in right hand. The left hand also held something out but is now broken off. The right leg, broken at bottom, extended straight down; the left leg was swung back at the knee. A section of the left leg has been removed and the foot re-attached higher than it belongs, thus giving an awkward impression.

139. A terracotta figurine of Men on horseback, acquired 1965 by McDaniel Collection, Harvard University.
Dimensions: Height 17.2 cm.

> Bibliography: Sotheby and Co., *Catalogue of Egyptian, Near Eastern, Greek, and Roman Antiquities*, May 17, 1965, p. 46, no. 193; Hiesinger, *op. cit.*, p. 307-8 and Plate IV; Lane II, p. 46, no. 11.

Men is shown riding right on a horse with upraised left forefoot. Men's head and upper body are turned to face the viewer. Men's costume is much the usual, this time with long leggings. He has a fat, cheerful face, which seems to be reflected in happiness on the horse's part too. The back of the statuette is very sketchily rendered, with an air hole in the middle.

I take the opportunity offered here to group other items of uncertain provenience.

140. A terracotta figurine of Men seated, in the possession of the Akademisches Kunstmuseum of the University of Bonn.
Dimensions: Height 17.6 cm.

> Bibliography: *Antiken aus dem akademischen Kunstmuseum Bonn*, Düsseldorf, 1969, p. 77, no. 80 and Pl. 51.

Men is shown seated, right foot slightly raised, on a stool without a back, perhaps covered with a cloth. He wears boots, and a chiton belted high across the chest, as well as the usual Phrygian cap. He holds a patera in the outstretched right hand, and an indistinct object in the upraised left. There is a crescent moon behind his shoulders. The hair-do, the features of the face, and the modeling of the chest, all give this statuette a womanish appearance. There is a rooster in relief on the side of the seat, near the right foot.

141. A terracotta statuette showing Men standing with Phrygian cap and crescent at shoulders. In National Museum, Athens, according to Perdrizet.
Dimensions unavailable.

>Bibliography: Perdrizet, *BCH* XX, 1896, p. 72, fig. 3; Lane I, p. 15, no. 4.

142. A plaque of marble reported in 1898 as being in the British Museum, but not to be found there in 1962.
Dimensions unavailable.

>Bibliography: Daremberg-Saglio, III, ii, p. 1395, figure 4671 (attribution to Athens) [1]; T. Homolle, *BCH*, XXIII, 1899, p. 389 and Plate I; M. P. Nilsson, *Geschichte der Griechischen Religion*, II, Plate 13, no. 1; M. I. Rostovzeff, *op. cit.*, p. 256, Plate 46, no. 1; Lane, I, p. 25, no. 22.

The stone bears a relief of which the upper area is occupied by a bust of Men with hair in ringlets, on a large crescent. He wears a solar crown, which has a crescent in the middle, surmounted by another crescent on an oval ornament. On the left there are two 8-pointed stars and on the right, one. In the upper left and upper right corners, the inscription:

Μηνὶ   Πλουτο-
Σωτῆρι καὶ   δώτηι

The central area of the relief is framed by two torches on either side, such as are usually associated with the Eleusinian mysteries. In the middle there is a large bull's head with one central eye, on the horns of which rests a two-headed snake, which makes the balance-bar of a scale. Between the bull's horns and the snake, there is a sort of rudder (or cornucopia?) between two fruits (or solar disks?). From the left end of the balance hangs a cornucopia, which a snake climbs up. From the other end hang a quiver (or club?) and bow.

---

[1] If any local attribution is to be given to this piece, it should probably be to the area of Dorylaeum (Eskişehir), because of the importance of σωτηρία in the inscriptions of that area. But that is not much to go on.

Between the bull's head and the cornucopia there is a Pan's pipe, and between the quiver and the bull's head, there is a pruning hook (or sacrificial implement?). Directly under the cornucopia, there are the caps of the Dioscuri, and under the quiver, the wheel (of Nemesis?). From either side of the bull's nose there springs a rudder (or meat-cleaver) out diagonally downwards. Between the left rudder and the Dioscuri-caps, there are tongs; between the right rudder and the wheel, a winged mirror. Directly under the bull's nose, there is a platter with pine-cone and leaves, borne by a figure of which the bare upper part of the body alone is visible.

In the bottom are, left to right, a caduceus, a small bull's head, grain, leaves, and unidentifiable fruit, all over a sheep; a long-legged waterbird, a pine-cone, and a crow, and over the pine-cone a goat, from behind which rises the figure holding the platter; a lion, a squid (goat's head?), a snake, and an indistinct object (whip?). The whole area is liberally scattered with small crescent moons, of which one can easily count more than twenty.

Dereköy (marked Bostan on map), Turkey
N.E. of Seydişehir

143. "Diminutive sarcophagus" in the court of a house, discovered by Sterrett in 1885.
Dimensions unknown.

Bibliography: Sterrett, *Wolfe Expedition*, p. 174, no. 284; Drexler, *op. cit.*, col. 2719-20; Perdrizet, *op. cit.*, p. 68, no. 1; Lane, I, pp. 45-46, no. 1.

The stone bears the following inscription:

['Η δεῖνα] 'Αραμόου ἑαυτῇ καὶ ἀνδρὶ μνήμης χάριν, ἐνο-
[ρκιζόμεθα δ]ὲ Μῆνα καταχθόνιον εἰς τοῦτο μνημεῖον μηδένα εἰσελθεῖν.

Fasıllar (Fassılar, Fassıler) E. of Beyşehir, Turkey

144. Low sarcophagus carved out of cliff in necropolis on height N.W. of village. Discovered by Jüthner and Patsch in 1902.

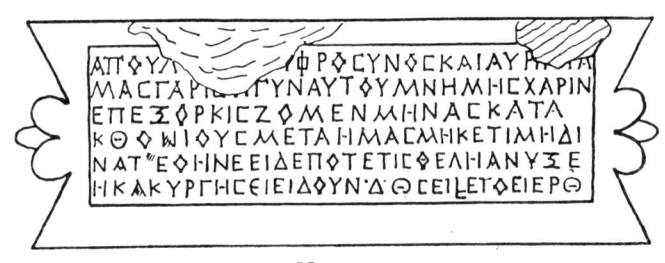

No. 144

Dimensions: 45 cm. inside height, letters 3 to 4 cm.

Bibliography: H. Swoboda, J. Keil, and F. Knoll, *Denkmäler aus Lykaonien, Pamphylien, und Isaurien*, Prague, 1935, p. 18, no. 18; Lane, I, p. 46, no. 1a.

The stone bears the following inscription within a decorated tabula, to the left and right of which there is a wreath:

Ἀπουλ[ήιος Ε]ὐφρόσυνος καὶ Αὐρη[λ]ία
Μάσγαρις ἡ γυν(ὴ) αὐτοῦ μνήμης χάριν.
Ἐπεξορκίζομεν Μῆνας κατα-
χθονίους μετὰ ἡμᾶς μηκέτι μηδί-
να τεθῆνε. Εἰ δέ ποτέ τις θέλῃ ἀνῦξε
ἢ κακυργήσει εἰδούν, δώσει ⊢ ε' τῶ εἱερῶ

⊢ = δηνάρια

Iconium: Konya, Turkey

145. Tetragonal cippus discovered by Sterrett in 1884 in house of Dr. Diamantides.

Dimensions unknown.

Bibliography: Sterrett, *Epigraphical Journey* (Papers of the American School, II, 1883-4) p. 200, no. 211; Drexler, *op. cit.*, col. 2725; Perdrizet, *op. cit.*, p. 69, no. 5; Lane I p. 46, no. 2.

The stone bears the following inscription:

Μ. Οὔλπιος Ἡρ[ά-]
κλειτος ἑαυ[τῷ]
καὶ Κλαυδίᾳ γυν-
[α]ικὶ αὐτοῦ καὶ τέ-
κνοις αὐτῶν τὴν

[λ]άρνακα καὶ τὸν β[ω-]
μὸν, ἄλλῳ δὲ μὴ θ-
εῖναι. Ὁ δ' ἐὰν ἐ-
[π]ισβιάσηται ἢ
ἀ[δ]ικήσει ἔχοιτο
[Μ]ῆνα Καταχθόνι-
ον κεχολωμέ-
νον.

146. Stone discovered in April/May of 1885 by G. Radet and P. Paris built into one of the towers at north bottom of the Acropolis. By 1902 in garden of Konya Museum. Not visible there in 1969—perhaps in storage.

Dimensions: Height 50 cm., width 38 cm., letters 3 cm.

> Bibliography: Drexler, *op. cit.*, col. 2725; G. Radet and P. Paris, *BCH*, X, 1886, p. 503, no. 6; Perdrizet, *op. cit.*, p. 69, no. 6; H. S. Cronin, *JHS*, XXII, 1902, p. 118, no. 42; G. Mendel, *BCH*, XXVI, 1902, p. 217, no. 8; W. H. Buckler et al., *JRS*, XIV, 1924, p. 47 bottom; Lane I, p. 46, no. 4.

The stone bears the following inscription:

[· · · · · · · · ·Ἐλευ-]
θερος [τῇ γυ-]
ναικὶ Τιεί[ᾳ μνή-]
μης χάριν.
Ἐάν τις τὴν στήλην
ἀδικήσει, κεχολω-
μένον ἔχοιτο
Μῆνα καταχθό-
νιον.

147. Stone of unknown type found at Konya (?) in 1902 (?) by W. M. Ramsay.

Dimensions unknown.

> Bibliography: H. S. Cronin, *JHS*, XXII, 1902, pp. 346-7, no. 82; Lane, I, p. 46, no. 5.

The stone bears the following inscription:

Λάρκιο[ς················]
ζῶν ἑαυ[τῷ καὶ τῇ γυναικὶ]
Πωσίλλῃ [καὶ τοῖς τέκνοις]
τὴν σο[ρὸν κατεσκεύασεν.]
Ἐνορκῶ [δὲ Μῆνα Καταχθόνιον]
καὶ θεοὺς [καταχθονίους μη-]
δένα ἀδικ[ήσειν τὸ μνῆμα μη-]
δὲ ἐπεισ[ενεγκεῖν σῶμα, ὃς δ']
ἂν ἐπεισε[νέγκῃ ἢ ἀδικήσῃ, δώσει]
τῷ φίσκῳ [δηνάρια δισχίλια]
πεντακόσ[ια καὶ ἕξει Μῆνα κε-]
χολωμένο[ν.]

148. Stone of unknown type found by Cronin in Araplar, a neighborhood (?) of Konya, in 1902 (?).
Dimensions unknown.

Bibliography: Cronin, *op. cit.*, p. 356, no. 112; Lane, I, p. 46, no. 6.

The stone bears the following inscription (line division obscure in publication):

[Δο]ύδης Μ[ενεδήμου·········Πα]τροκλεῖ τῷ ἀνδρὶ
αὐτῆς τὸν κείονα ἀνέστησεν, μ(νήμης) χ(άριν),
[······]τος καὶ Τείμονα θρεπτοὺς αὐτοῦ
[······] ἐλεύθερον [·············]
Ὁρκίσζω Μῆνα Καταχθόνιον μηδένα [ἕτερον]
[ἐσενεχθῆναι] εἰ μὴ μόνον τὴν δούλην μου [········]

149. Limestone stele, broken across top (originally with pediment). In center of front, sunken panel with text. Above, figure of a man left, woman right. Woman has left elbow propped on right hand, her head defaced. First seen by Ramsay and W. M. Calder in excavations of Alaeddin, Konya in 1910. Not visible in museum in 1969—perhaps in storage—although Calder and Buckler report that it was housed there.

Dimensions: Height 1.35 m., width at top 51 cm., at bottom 56 cm., thickness 24 cm.

Bibliography: W. M. Calder, *Revue de Philologie*, XXXVI, 1912, p. 66, no. 33; W. H. Buckler et al., *JRS*, XIV, 1924, p. 47, no. 37 and Plate VIII; *SEG*, VI, 1932, p. 76, no. 427; Ramsay, *Social Basis*, p. 30, no. 21; Lane, II, p. 46, no. 1a.

The stone bears the following inscription:

Αὖλος Ἰούλι-
ος Φιλήμων κ-
αὶ Ἰουλία Μα-
μάθια Δάφν-
ῳ υἱῷ
μνήμης χά-
ριν. Ὅς δ' ἂν ἀ-
δικήσῃ τὴν σ-
τήλην ἢ ἀ-
ποκόψει ἕξει
τὸν Μῆνα κε-
χολωμένον
τὸν Καταχθόνι-
ον.

150. Stone of unknown type first seen by Prodromos Petrides in 1910 in Alaeddin excavations. Calder implies that it was taken to Konya museum. Not visible there in 1969.

Dimensions unavailable.

Bibliography: Calder, *op. cit.*, p. 65, no. 30; Lane, II, p. 46, no. 1b.

The stone bears the following inscription:

Μ. Αἴλιος Ὀκ[τ]ά-
ουιος ἑαυτῷ
ζῶν καὶ γυναικὶ
Δομνίλλῃ καὶ
τέκνοις ἐποίησεν
τὴν λάρνακα καὶ
τὸν βωμὸν, ἑτέρῳ
δὲ μηδενὶ ἐξὸν
εἶναι εἰσενεχθ[ῆ-]
ναι. Ἐὰν δέ τις ἐ-

πεισβιάσηται
ἔχοιτο Μῆνα Κα-
ταχθόνιον κε-
χολωμένον.

151. Sepulchral stone in walls of Iconium seen by Seetzen in 1803 (?)
Dimensions unknown.
> Bibliography: *CIG*, 4008; Ramsay, *JHS*, XXXVIII, 1918, p. 168, no. X; Lane, I, p. 47, no. 9.

The stone bears the following inscription (Ramsay's restoration):

Ἐάν τις ἀδικήσει τὴ-
[ν] ἱστήλην Ἑρμίου [κεχολω-]
[μένον ἐχ]έτω [Μ]ῆνα χθό[ν]ιο[ν].
Ἀνέστησεν δὲ Μάν-
ης υἱῷ.

152. A stone of unknown description copied in Konya (Museum ?), in 1902 by Ramsay. (Not seen in Museum in 1969).
Dimensions unknown.
> Bibliography: Cronin, *JHS*, XXII, 1902, p. 125, no. 59; Lane, I, p. 47, no. 10.

The stone bears the following inscription:

Ἀκύλας
ΜΕΝΙΔΣΚΟ
Μηνὶ εὐχήν.

153. Limestone altar with upper and lower mouldings, upper front corners broken. Seen by W. H. Buckler in Konya Museum in June, 1924, for first time, and still there in 1969. Said to be from the environs of Konya.
Dimensions: Height 52 cm., width 31 cm., thickness 31 cm.
> Bibliography: W. H. Buckler et al., *JRS*, XIV, 1924, p. 25, no. 1; *JRS*, XVIII, 1928, p. 38, bottom; *SEG*, VI, p. 71, no. 401; Ramsay, *Social Basis*, p. 151, no. 154; Lane, I, p. 48, no. 2; Lane, II, p. 47.

The stone bears on the front a relief of a bust of Men on a pedestal.

On either side a snake in relief rises up to rest its head on top of the altar. On the top, a snake lies coiled. The following inscription is arranged with the top line on the upper moulding, the rest around the bust:

[···]Ν[········]
ου   Ἁδρια-
νοπο   λείτη-
ς θε   ῷ
Οὐ   ιν-
διει   νῷ
εὐ   χήν.

Lystra: Hatunsaray, Turkey

154. Stone of unknown description, found by Sterrett in 1885, in the Eastern Cemetery.
Dimensions unknown.

> Bibliography: Sterrett, *Wolfe Expedition*, p. 146, no. 251; Drexler, *op. cit.*, col. 2726; Perdrizet, *op. cit.*, p. 69, no. 4; Ramsay, *Social Basis*, p. 196, no. 204; Lane, I, p. 46, no. 3.

The stone bears the following inscription (Ramsay's restoration):

> [Π. Καλου]ίσιος ζ[ῶ]ν φρονῶν ἐπόησεν ἑαυτῷ
> [καὶ Βάδ]ι τῇ ἰδ[ίᾳ] γυναικὶ μνήμης ἕνεκεν.
> [Ὅς δ' ἂν ἀδ]ικήσῃ τὸ μνῆμα, Μῆνα ἄνωθεν καὶ κάτο-
> [θεν κεχολωμένους ἔχοιτο.]

Area of ancient *Savatra:* Ennek, Turkey

155. Stone of uncertain description, found by T. A. Callander, 1904, built into the doorway of a hut.
Dimensions unknown.

> Bibliography: Callander, *Studies in the History and Art of the Eastern Provinces of the Roman Empire* (Aberdeen University Studies, XX, 1906), p. 160, no. 9; H. Swoboda et al., *Denkmäler*, p. 18; Lane, I, p. 46, no. 7.

The stone bears the following inscription:

Διαδούμε-
νος ἑαυτῷ καὶ
Ἡλιάδι τῇ συνβ[ί-]
ῳ τὸν βωμὸν
καὶ τὴν στήλην
καὶ τὰ πέλτα, καὶ
ἐνορκῶ τρῖς θ[εοὺς]
Μῆνας ἀνεπιλύ[τως]
μηδένα ἕτερον ἐ-
πεισενεχθῆναι ἢ
μόνην Ἀρτεμεισίαν τὴν
ἐμήν.

Area of ancient *Sidamaria:* Kaleköy, Turkey

156. Heavy stone used as doorstep discovered by Callander in 1904.
Dimensions: 6 ft. by 2 ft. by 1 ft.
Bibliography: Callander, *op. cit.*, p. 164, no. 23; Swoboda et al., *op. cit.*, p. 18; Lane, I, p. 47, no. 8.

The stone bears the following inscription:

[Ἀ]θηνα[ῖος καὶ Νει-]
κομήδης, υἱο[ὶ] Νεικά-
νορος, Νεικάνορα
Ἀθηναίου τὸν ἑαυτῶν
πατέρα καὶ Τάττιν Τα-
τέου[ς] γ' Νεικομήδους
τὴν μητέρα αὐτῶν,
οἱ κτίσαντες τὸν τά-
φον εὐνοίας ἕνεκεν,
ἐνορκίζω δὲ Μῆ-
νας τόν τε Οὐράνι-
ον καὶ τοὺς Κατα-

χθονίους μὴ ἐξ[εῖ-]
ναί τινι πολῆσαι
τὸ περίβολον τοῦ
τά[φ]ου, μήτε ἀγορά-
ζειν ἐκτὸ[ς] το[ῦ]
[ἀδελφοῦ.]

Androna (?): Topaklı, Turkey, S.W. of Ankara

157. Small altar stone found by J. G. C. Anderson in summer of 1898 in floor of mosque.
Dimensions unknown.

```
   ❋  ⟨ΜΗΘΝΙ⟩ ✿
      ⟨ΑΝΔΡΩ⟩ ΝΗ
 ΝΩ
      ΤΡΟΠΟΣΚΑΙΒΕΛ
         ΛΑΕΥΧΗΝ
```

No. 157

Bibliography: J. G. C. Anderson, *JHS*, XIX, 1899, p. 96, no. 76; Lane, I, p. 48, no. 1.

The stone bears an incised decoration of a crescent moon and three flowers, one inside the horns of the moon and one on either side. The following inscription is arranged with the first line and the first five letters of the second within the horns of the moon, the rest outside. In addition, the first line is broken in the middle by one of the flowers:

Μη νὶ
'Ανδρω νη-
νῷ
Τρόπος καὶ Βέλ-
λα εὐχήν.

Area of *Ancyra*: Ankara, Turkey

158. Plaque of white marble, curved behind, with relief, first seen by L. Robert before 1955 in Ankara museum. Exact provenience unknown.
Dimensions: Height 50 cm., width 52 cm., thickness 17 cm.
> Bibliography: L. Robert, *Hellenica*, X, 1955, p. 15 and Plate IV; Lane, I, p. 48, no. 3.

Between two pilasters that apparently supported an arch, we see a bust of Men, drapery held by a pin at right shoulder, battered face, Phrygian cap, and crescent at shoulders.

159. Statuette in the round of Men on horseback of white marble. Seen by L. Robert at same time, same uncertainty as to origin. Horse's legs are broken off.
Dimensions: Preserved height (?) 13 cm., maximum width (?) 14 cm.
> Bibliography: L. Robert, *Hellenica*, X, 1955, pp. 15-16 and Plate XXX.

Men is portrayed riding right and turning to face the viewer. Usual costume and crescent. In his right hand he holds a pine-cone.

Antiocheia Pisidiae: Yalvaç, Turkey

160. Small round cippus found in 1912 at the shrine of Men Askaenos, east of Antioch.
Dimensions unknown.
> Bibliography: G. L. Cheesman, *JRS*, III, 1913, p. 258, no. 3; *Année Epigraphique*, 1914, p. 373, no. 261; Lane, I, p. 30, no. 3 (with interpretation of *LVS* as *Luno* (or *-ae*) *votum solvit* and fact that in my opinion it establishes connection with Men).

The stone bears the following inscription:

LVS

Ti. Claudiu[s]
Epinicus

Proc(urator) et Prae-
gustator et
a secretis Aug(usti)
VIir aug(ustalis) c(oloniae) c(aesariae)
d(ecreto) d(ecurionum) ex mandatu
Caristianor(um)
Droserae et
Mileti parenti-
um suorum
posuit.

161. Fragment of an inscription found in 1912 in the same sanctuary. Apparently complete on top, bottom and left.

Dimensions: Height approximately 40 cm., width approximately 20 cm., letters line 1, 2.7 cm.

Bibliography: J. G. C. Anderson, *JRS*, III, 1913, p. 269, no. 2; Lane, I, p. 40, no. 6.

The inscription reads, as best I can figure from the photograph of the squeeze, as follows:

στ[έφανος]
σ
ἱερεὺς θ[εοῦ Μηνὸς καὶ θεᾶς]
Δήμητ[ρος ·············]
[π]άντα [τὸν βίον ········]
Λυσιμαχ[···············]
στεφαν[················]
ἱερεὺς τὸ δ' [············]

162. Tablet of which five fragments were found in the excavation of 1912 in the sanctuary. Now in Archaeological Museum of Konya.

Dimensions: As put together in plaster in the museum, height 39.5 cm., width 24 cm.

Bibliography: J. G. C. Anderson, *op. cit.*, p. 271, no. 6; *Année Épigraphique*, 1914, p. 374; Lane, I, p. 30, no. 9.

The tablet contains the pentameter line:

Ἀσκαίης ναέτην Μῆνα σέβων ἐθέμην.

arranged in such a way that reading from A in the center out on any zigzag you get the sentence (concentric lozenges of letters).

163. A bomos with defaced top found by Calder and Ramsay in 1911, built into a house wall in Abucılar, a district of Yalvaç.
Dimensions: unknown.

Bibliography: W. M. Calder, *JRS*, II, 1912, p. 93, no. 22; Lane, I, p. 31, no. 10.

The stone bears, below the inscription, a relief of an eagle flying with a wreath in its claws. The inscription reads as follows:

Στήλην τοι καὶ τοῦτον ἐπευχάδιον θέτο βωμ[ὸν]
Πρωτίων Ἀσκαίης τῶι μεδέοντι θεῶι,
τὸν Μοῦσαι θρέψαντο, σὺ δ' ὦ παροδεῖτα προσεύ[ξαι]
χαίρων καὶ σπένδ' εὖ σαῖσιν ἐπ' εὐτυχίαι[ς]

164. Hexagonal column with slightly concave sides and moulded top. Found in 1912 toward northern end of cistern in sanctuary.
Dimensions: Letters 2.9 cm.; from picture, height 1.04 cm., width of inscribed face 24 cm.

Bibliography: Anderson, *JRS*, III, 1913, p. 287, no. 12 and figure 62; Lane, I, p. 33, no. 17.

The column bears the following inscription:

Ἐπὶ ἀγωνο-
θέτου Γ. Οὐλ-
πίου Βαιβια-
νοῦ αὔγου-
ρ(ος) καὶ ἱερέως
[δ]ιὰ βίου τοῦ
[πα]τρίου θε-
[οῦ] Μηνὸς
[καὶ] θεᾶς Δή-
[μητρ]ος Τιβ.
Κλαύδιον
Μαρκιανὸν
νεικήσαν-
τα πάλην, ὃν

ASIA MINOR

ἀποδυσάμε-
νον παρητή-
[σ]αντο οἱ ἀν-
[ταγ]ωνισταί.
Traces of another line.

165. Hexagonal column broken below found in same place as preceding in 1912.

Dimensions: Letters 2.8 cm., from picture, height 75 cm., width of inscribed face 19.6 cm.

> Bibliography: J. G. C. Anderson, *op. cit.*, p. 288, no. 13 and figure 63; Lane, I, p. 33, no. 18.

The stone bears the following inscription:

Ἐπὶ ἀγωνο-
θέτου διὰ βί-
ου Γ. Οὐλπί-
ου Βαιβια-
νοῦ αὔγου-
ρος καὶ ἱερέ-
ως διὰ βίου
τοῦ πατρίου
θεοῦ Μηνὸς
καὶ θεᾶς Δή-
μητρος Λ.
Πλώτιον
Μαρκιαν-
[όν · · · · · · ·]

166. Hexagonal column found at same time at the south end of cistern.

Dimensions: Letters 2.8 cm., height (Anderson) 1.50 m., according to picture, 1.47 cm., inscribed face width, according to picture, 20.8 cm.

> Bibliography: J. G. C. Anderson, *op. cit.*, p. 288, no. 14 and Plate XXI; *Année Épigraphique*, 1914, p. 374, no. 263; Lane, I, p. 33, no. 19.

The stone bears the following inscription:

Ἐπὶ ἀγωνο-

θέτου διὰ
βίου Γ. Οὐλπί-
ου Βαιβιανοῦ
αὔγουρ(ος) καὶ
ἱερέως διὰ βί-
ου τοῦ πατρί-
ου θεοῦ Μη-
νὸς καὶ θεᾶς
Δήμητρος
Γναῖον Δότ-
τιον Μάγνον
νεικήσαν-
τα σαλπι-
κτὰς ἀγῶ-
να Μαξιμι-
άνειον ἡ
πατρὶς
θέμιδι β′.

167. Similar hexagonal column, found in same place.

Dimensions: Letters 2.8 cm., height, according to picture, 1.45 m., inscribed face 23.2 cm.

Bibliography: J. G. C. Anderson, *op. cit.*, p. 289, no. 16 and Plate XXII; Lane, I, p. 33, no. 21.

The stone bears the following inscription:

Ἐπὶ ἀγωνο-
θέτου διὰ
βίου Γ. Οὐλ-
πίου Βαιβι-
ανοῦ αὔγου(ρος)
καὶ ἱερέως
διὰ βίου τοῦ
πατρίου θε-
οῦ Μηνὸς καὶ
θε(ᾶς) Δήμητρος
Ἰούλιον Κόρ-

διον Θεόδω-
ρον νεική-
σαντα πάλην
ἀγῶνα Μα-
ξιμιάνειον
ἡ πατρὶς Θέ-
μιδι ζ'.

168. A plain slab built into the wall of the Kuşku mezarlık in Yalvaç in 1912.

Dimensions unknown.

Bibliography: J. G. C. Anderson, *op. cit.*, p. 289, no. 17 and fig. 65; Lane, I, p. 33, no. 22.

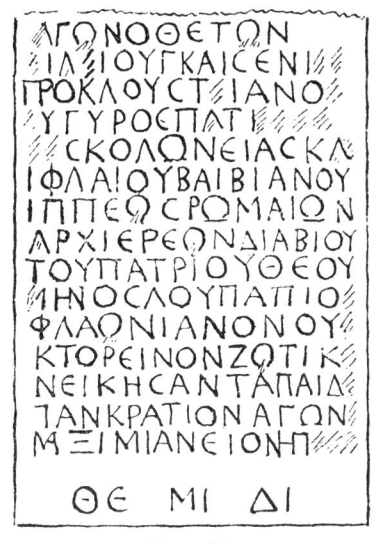

No. 168

The stone bears the following inscription:

Ἀγωνοθετο(ύ)ν[των]
[δ]ιὰ [β]ίου Γ. Καισενγ[ίου]
Πρόκλου Στ[α]ιανο[ῦ]
[α]ὔγουρος, πάτρ[ωνος]

[τῆ]ς κολωνείας κα[ὶ]
Γ. Φλαίου Βαιβιανοῦ
ἱππέως Ῥωμαίων
ἀρχιερέως διὰ βίου
τοῦ πατρίου θεοῦ
Μηνὸς Λού(κιον) Πάπιο[ν]
Φλαο(υ)ιανὸν Οὐ[ι]-
κτορεῖνον Ζωτικ[ὸν]
νεικήσαντα παίδ[ων]
πανκράτιον ἀγῶν[α]
Μαξιμιάνειον ἡ π[ατρὶς]
Θέμιδι.

169. Plaque found in 1912 in a mosque in northern extremity of Yalvaç.

Dimensions: Letters ca. 2.5 cm., height according to picture 32.5 cm., width according to picture 22.5 cm.

> Bibliography: J. G. C. Anderson, *op. cit.*, p. 290, no. 18 and fig. 66; Lane, I, p. 34, no. 23.

The stone bears the following inscription:

['Ἀγωνοθετούντων]
[. . . . .]
[. . . . πάτρωνος τῆς]
κολωνείας
καὶ Γ. Φλαῖου Βα[ι-]
βιανοῦ ἱππ[έως]
Ῥωμαίων ἀρχι[ε-]
ρέως διὰ βίου
τοῦ πατρίου
Θεοῦ Μηνὸ[ς]
[Λ.] Ἰούλιον Λό-
[μ]νον νει[κήσαντα]
. . . .

170. Tetragonal column with upper and lower mouldings found at north end of cistern in sanctuary in 1912.

Dimensions: Letters of line 2, 2.3 cm., height according to picture 1.36 m., width of inscribed face (shaft) ca. 40 cm., width of upper moulding 44 cm.

Bibliography: J. G. C. Anderson, *op. cit.*, p. 291, no. 19, Plate XXIII; Lane, I, p. 34, no. 24.

The stone bears the following inscription, of which the first line is on the upper moulding, the rest on the shaft (the last line is in smaller letters):

        Ἀγαθῇ Τύχῃ.
        Ἀγωνοθετούντων
        διὰ βίου Γ. Καισεννί-
        ου Πρόκλου Σταια-
        νοῦ αὔγουρος πάτρω-
        νος τῆς κολωνείας
        καὶ Γ. Φλαίου Βαιβια-
        νοῦ ἱππέως Ῥωρωμαί-
        ων ἀρχιερέως διὰ βίου
        τοῦ πατρίου θεοῦ Μη-
        νὸς Τερέντιον Οὔλ-
        πιον Ζώσιμον νεική-
        σαντα παίδων παν-
        κράτιον καὶ δι(α)βιβάσαν-
        τα κλήρους β' ἀγῶνα
        Μαξιμιάνειον ἡ πατρὶς
            θέμιδι
        ὑπὸ ἐπιστάτην Ἰούλιον Δόμνον.

171. Round cippus found in 1912 inside N.W. wall of sanctuary. Dimensions: Letters line 2, 3.2 cm.

Bibliography: J. G. C. Anderson, *op. cit.*, p. 291, no. 20 and fig. 67; Lane, I, p. 34, no. 25.

The stone bears the following inscription:

        Ἀγαθῇ Τύχῃ.
        Ἀγωνοθετοῦντος
        διὰ βίου Γ. Φλ. Βαιβια-
        νοῦ ποντίφικος ⳨
        ἱππέως Ῥωμαίων

πάτρων(ος) τῆς κολωνείας
ἀρχιερέως διὰ βίου τοῦ πατρίου θεοῦ Μηνὸς Τε-
ρέντιον Οὔλπιον Μάρ-
κελλον νεικήσαν-
τα παίδων πανκράτιον
ἀγῶνα Μαξιμιάνει-
ον διαβιβάσαντα κλή-
ρους β' ἡ πατρὶς
 Θέμιδι
ὑπὸ ἐπιστάτην Ἰούλιον
 Δόμνον

ΑΓΑΘΗ ΤΥΧΗ

ΑΓΩΝΟΘΕΤΟΥΝΤΟΣ
ΔΙΑΒΙΟΥ Γ. ΦΛ. ΒΑΙΒΙΑ
ΝΟΥ ΠΟΝΤΙΦΙΚΟΣ ΙΒ᾽
ΙΠΠΕΩΣ ΡΩΜΑΙΩΝ
ΠΑΤΡΩΝ ΗΣ ΚΟΛΩΝΙΑΣ
ΑΡΧΙΕΡΕΩΣ ΔΙΑΒΙΟΥ ΤΟΥ ΠΑ
ΤΡΙΟΥ ΘΕΟΥ ΜΗΝΟΣ ΤΕ
ΡΕΝΤΙΟΝ ΟΥΛΠΙΟΝ ΜΑΡ
ΚΕΛΛΟΝ · ΝΕΙΚΗΣΑΝ
ΤΑ ΠΑΙΔΩΝ ΠΑΝΚΡΑΤΙΟΝ
ΑΓΩΝΑ ΜΑΞΙΜΙΑΝΕΙ
ΟΝ ΔΙΑΒΙΒΑΣΑΝΤΑ ΚΛΗ
ΡΟΥΣ · Β' Η ΠΑΤΡΙΣ ·

ΘΕΜΙΔΙ

ΥΠΟ ΕΠΙΣΤΑΤΗΝ ΙΟΥΛΙΟΝ
 ΔΟΜΝΟΝ

No. 171

172. Thin round cippus found in 1912 inside N.W. wall of sanctuary.

Dimensions: Letters in line 2, 2.7 to 2.8 cm., height according to picture 91 cm., diameter according to picture 31.5 cm.

> Bibliography: J. G. C. Anderson, *op. cit.*, p. 293, no. 21 and figure 68; Lane, I, p. 34, no. 26.

The stone bears the following inscription:

>> Ἀγ[αθῇ] Τύ[χη]
>> Ἀγωνοθετοῦντος
>> διὰ βίου Γ. Φλαιουίου
>> Βαιβιανοῦ ποντίφικος
>> ἱππέως Ῥωμαίων πατρω-
>> νος τῆς κολωνείας
>> ἀρχιερέως διὰ βίου
>> τοῦ πατρίου θεοῦ Μηνὸς
>> Καλπούρνιον Μάγιον
>> Εὐτύχην νεικήσαντα
>> νεικήσαντα παίδων
>> πάλην ἀγῶνα Μαξιμιά-
>> νειον ἡ πατρὶς
>>   θέμιδι.

173. Cippus broken below found in north end of cistern in sanctuary in 1912.

Dimensions: Letters 2.8 to 3 cm., height according to picture 52.8 cm., diameter according to picture 40 cm., diameter according to Anderson 1′ 3″.

> Bibliography: J. G. C. Anderson, *op. cit.*, p. 293, no. 22 and figure 69; Lane, I, p. 34, no. 27.

The stone bears the following inscription:

>> Ἀγωνοθετοῦντος διὰ
>> βίου Γ. Φλαίου Βαιβιανοῦ
>> ποντίφικος ἱππέως
>> Ῥωμαίων πάτρωνος
>> τῆς κολωνείας ἀρχι-
>> ερέως διὰ βίου πα-

τρίου θεοῦ Μηνὸς
Τερέντιον Οὔλπιον
Ζώσιμον νεικήσαν-
[τα............]

174. Drum of an Ionic column (?), found in 1912 in the N. end of the cistern in the sanctuary. A panel for the inscription has been made by smoothing away the fluting on one side.

Dimensions: Letters, average 3 cm., height, judging by photograph, 91 cm., diameter bottom, by photograph, 45.5 cm., diameter top, by photograph, 39.9 cm., circumference, by Anderson, 5′ 1/2″.

Bibliography: J. G. C. Anderson, *op. cit.*, p. 294-5, no. 23 and figure 70; *Année Épigraphique*, 1914, p. 374, no. 264; Lane, I, p. 34, no. 28.

The stone bears the following inscription:

Ἐπὶ ἀγωνοθέτου
διὰ βίου Γ. Φλ. Βαιβι-
ανοῦ ποντίφικος
ἱππέως Ῥωμαί-
ων πάτρωνος τῆς
κολωνείας ἀρχιερέ-
ως διὰ βίου τοῦ πατρί-
ου θεοῦ Μηνὸς
Μᾶρ(κον) Οὐείρειον Μαρ-
κιανὸν νεικήσαντα
παίδων πάλην
ἀγῶνα Μαξιμιά-
νειον θέμιδι τὸ
δεύτερον ἡ πα-
τρὶς δια(βι)βάσαντα κλήρους ζ′,
κριθέντα Πύθεια ἐν Ἀν-
κύρᾳ καὶ ἀγωνισάμε-
νον ἐνδόξως.

Of the various fragments that Anderson publishes as 24-25, the only one that seems to have any bearing is 24b:

[θ]εοῦ Μηνό[ς]

175. Statuette of white marble, found in the sanctuary of Men at Yalvaç in 1912, now in the museum of Constantinople.

Dimensions: Height 29.5 cm., of which four for the plinth.

Bibliography: Mendel, *Catalogue*, III, p. 591, no. 1380; J. G. C. Anderson, *op. cit.*, p. 274-6 and figure 54; Lane, I, p. 35, no. 31.

No. 175

Men is shown standing, draped, with his left arm resting on a pillar. The left hand is broken—it may have held an attribute. The head, and crescent, are likewise broken off, as is the right arm, which was raised to hold a staff, of which traces are visible on the plinth. The left foot is raised to be set on a bucranium. The right leg is broken between the bottom of the drapery and the foot, attached to the plinth. Also visible on the plinth are the feet of a rooster, near the bottom of the staff. There are traces of the staff also on the right hip.

176. Votive stele with lug at bottom, found (in sanctuary?) in 1912, now in museum at Constantinople.

Dimensions: Height 53.5 cm. (of which 8.5 are for the lug), width at bottom 24 cm., width at top of arch over niche, 18.2 cm., width of upper moulding 21 cm., thickness 5 to 8 cm., height of niche 16.7 cm., height of letters 1.2 to 2 cm.

Bibliography: Mendel, *Catalogue*, III, p. 592, no. 1381; J. G. C. Anderson, *op. cit.*, p. 273 and Plate XX; Lane, I, p. 35, no. 32.

The stele has a pediment with acroteria above (vegetable decoration connecting acroteria) and a rosette in the middle of the pediment. The main field is occupied by a niche (on either side of which, above, there is a star with six points), in which there is a bust of Men with Phrygian cap and crescent at shoulders. He wears a sleeved tunic and a chlamys held by a pin on the right shoulder. He has a slightly melancholy expression. Under the niche, the inscription:

Sex(tus) Flavonius Naevius
LVS

177. Stele of white marble broken in 14 fragments. Found 1912 in sanctuary of Yalvaç. Now in museum of Constantinople.

Dimensions: Height 1.145 m., width at bottom 58.8 cm., width halfway up column 56.4 cm., width of upper moulding 59 cm., height of columns 65 cm., thickness 3.5 to 4 cm., letters 2.4 to 3 cm.

Bibliography: Mendel, *Catalogue*, III, no. 1382, p. 592-3; Lane, I, p. 35, no. 33.

The stele has a pediment and acroteria, a vegetative ornament connecting the acroteria, and a circular ornament in the middle of the pediment. Dentils on both horizontal and raking cornices. The main field is contained between two Corinthian columns and shows, towards the top, two crescents, and at bottom, a bull tied to a flaming altar by a rope around its horns. The bull on the left faces the altar on right. The bull is on a plinth. The main field bears the following inscription:

M. ⟅ Ἀγαθῇ Τύχῃ
‿   ‿
M. Οὐίρριος Γενού-
κιος Ἀντωνιανὸς
καὶ Μᾶρκος Οὐίρ-
ριος Γενούκιος

Σάνκτος Ἀντω-
νιανὸς τεκμορεύ-
σαντες Μηνὶ Πατρίῳ
εὐχήν.

No. 177

178. Stone (of unknown type) "in the wall of the Djami, inside the town, nearest the barracks at Yalvaç." First seen by W. Hamilton prior to 1842. Ampler text by Sterrett.

Dimensions unknown.

> Bibliography: W. I. Hamilton, *Researches in Asia Minor, Pontus, and Armenia*, London, 1842, no. 180; J. C. Orelli and W. Henzen, *Inscriptionum Latinarum Selectarum Amplissima Collectio* (vol. III, Zurich, 1856), no. 6157; Le Bas-Waddington, III, i, p. 446, no. 1818; *CIL*, III, (1873-1902), 295 and 6829; Sterrett, *Epigraphical Journey*, p. 129, no. 101; Ramsay, *Cities of St. Paul*, London, 1907, p. 286; *Social Basis*, p. 143, no. 148; Lane, I, p. 36, no. 34.

The stone bears the following inscription:

> C(aio) Albucio, C(aii) f(ilio)
> Ser(gia) Firmo, aed(ili),
> duumvir(o), qui pecuni-
> am destinavit per
> testamentum ad
> certamen gymnicum
> quotannis (f)acien-
> dum diebus festis
>   Lunae
> D(ecreto) D(ecurionum)

See Lane, *loc. cit.*, for justification of referring this to Men-cult.

The following inscriptions are all from the peribolos wall of the sanctuary of Men Askaenos above Pisidian Antioch, and all were published in *JHS*, XXXII, 1912, by Miss Margaret Hardie (Mrs. Hasluck). All are accompanied by line drawings, but the dimensions are never given.

179. Hardie, p. 121, no. 1, fig. 9.
Four naiskoi with crescents in field. Above all four:

> Μηνὶ εὐχήν.

Underneath each one, a name:

Α. Νερά-	Λ. Σέντιος	Γ. Οὐείβιος	Α. Νερά-
τιος Πόσ-	Μάξιμος	Οὐειτάλης	τιος Α-
τουμος			ρ······

For the second name, see no. 222.

ASIA MINOR

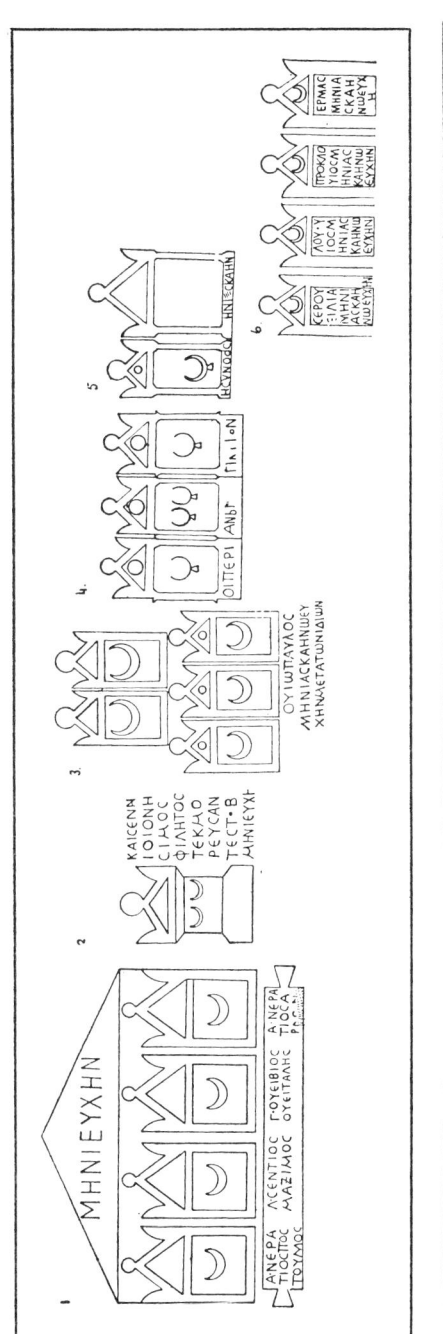

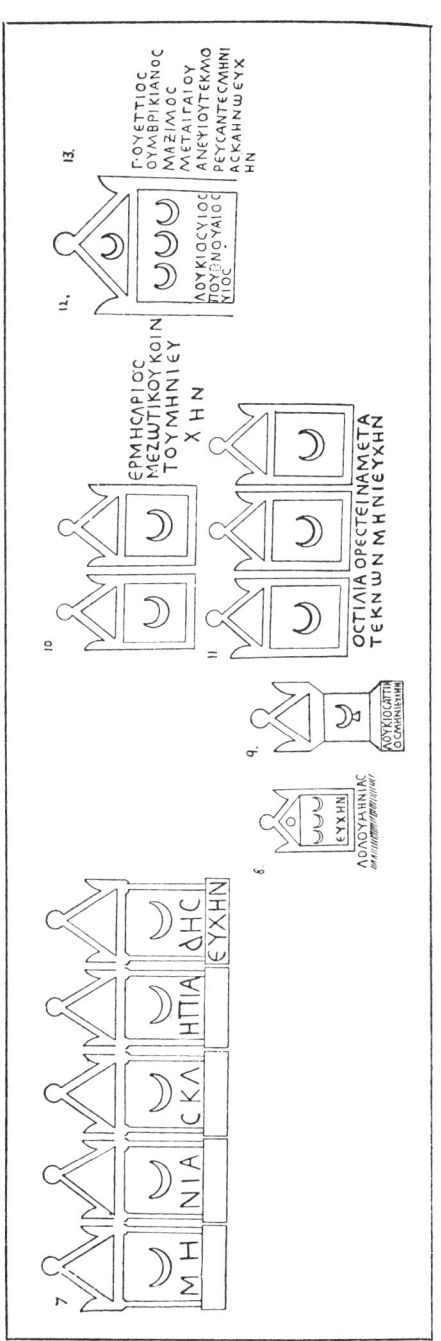

No. 179-191

180. Hardie, p. 123, no. 2 and fig. 9.

Imitation stele with two crescents in field, to right side, inscription:

> Καισένν-
> ιοι Ὀνή-
> σιμος
> Φίλητος
> τεκμο-
> ρεύσαν-
> τες τὸ β'
> Μηνὶ εὐχή[ν]

181. Hardie, p. 124, no. 3 and fig. 9; John Ferguson, *The Religions of the Roman Empire*, Ithaca, 1970, p. 217.

Five naiskoi, two above and three below (the three lower ones with circles in pediment), under all of which the inscription:

> Οὐίω Παῦλος
> Μηνὶ Ἀσκαηνῷ εὐ-
> χὴν μετὰ τῶν ἰδίων.

182. Hardie, p. 125, no. 4 and fig. 9.

Three naiskoi, with two lugged crescents in middle one, one each in side ones, circles in pediments. Across the bottoms of the naiskoi, the inscription:

> Οἱ περὶ Ἀν·····ον.

183. Hardie, p. 126, no. 5 and fig. 9.

Two naiskoi, in left of which a lugged crescent, and circle in pediment. Across bottoms of naiskoi, the inscription:

> Ἡ σύνοδο[ς Μ]ηνὶ [Ἀ]σκαην[ῷ].

184. Hardie, p. 126, no. 6 and fig. 9.

Four naiskoi, crescents in pediment, inscriptions in fields:

Σερου-	Λού(κιος) ὑ-	Πρόκλο[ς]	Ἑρμᾶς
ειλία	ιὸς Μ-	υἱὸς Μ-	Μηνὶ Ἀ-
Μηνὶ	ηνὶ Ἀσ-	ηνὶ Ἀσ-	σκαη-
Ἀσκαη-	καηνῷ	καηνῷ	νῷ εὐχ-
νῷ εὐχήν.	εὐχήν.	εὐχήν.	ή[ν].

185. Hardie, p. 126, no. 7 and fig. 9.

Five naiskoi, side by side, all with crescent in field. In the fields, below the crescents, and across bottom of no. 5:

> Μηνὶ Ἀσκληπιάδης
> εὐχήν.

186. Hardie, p. 126, no. 8 and fig. 9.

Naiskos with three crescents in field and circle in pediment; in the field below the crescents and below naiskos, the inscription:

> Εὐχὴν
> Λόλου Μηνὶ Ἀσ-
> [καηνῷ].

187. Hardie, p. 127, no. 9 and fig. 9.

Imitation stele with lugged crescent in field. Across the bottom, the inscription:

> Λούκιος Ἀττιῆ-
> ος Μηνὶ εὐχήν.

188. Hardie, p. 127, no. 10 and fig. 9.

Two naiskoi, crescent in field of each. To the right side, the inscription:

> Ἑρμῆς Ἄπριος
> με(τὰ) Ζωτικοῦ Κοίν-
> του Μηνὶ εὐ-
> χήν.

189. Hardie, p. 127, no. 11 and fig. 9.

Three naiskoi with crescents in field. Underneath:

> Ὁστιλία Ὀρεστεῖνα μετὰ
> τέκνων Μηνὶ εὐχήν.

190. Hardie, p. 127, no. 12 and fig. 9.

Naiskos with one crescent in pediment, three in field. Under the crescents, in the field, the inscription:

Λούκιος υἱὸς
Πουβνουαῖος
εὐχήν.

191. Hardie, p. 129, no. 13 and fig. 9.
Inscription alone:

Γ. Οὐέττιος
Οὐμβρικιανὸς
Μάξιμος
μεταὶ Γαίου
ἀνεψιοῦ τεκμο-
ρεύσαντες Μηνὶ
Ἀσκαηνῷ εὐχ-
ήν.

192. Hardie, p. 129, no. 14 and fig. 10.
Two naiskoi, side by side, with lugged crescents in field, circles in pediment. Across and below both fields, the inscription:

Αὐγμης Ἱλάρου
τεκμορεύ-
σας (μετὰ) θρεπ-
τοῦ Συντρόφου
Μηνὶ εὐχήν.

193. Hardie, p. 129, no. 15 and fig. 10; Ramsay, *JRS*, VIII, 1918, p. 109, with variant reading.
Naiskos with five crescents in field, circle in pediment. Below the crescents, in the field:

Μεινοδώ[ρ-]	Ἡ συνοδί-
α Μηνὶ εὐ-	α Μηνὶ εὐ-
χήν. (Hardie)	χήν. (Ramsay)

194. Hardie, p. 130, no. 16 and fig. 10.
Naiskos with three crescents in field after first line of inscription. Circle in pediment. Inscription across field, spilling into right and bottom margins:

ASIA MINOR

Ζώσιμ-
ος μετὰ τ-
έκνων
Μηνὶ Ἀσ-
καηνῷ εὐ-
χήν.

195. Hardie, p. 130, no. 17 and fig. 10 (only the first of the two items that follow); Ramsay, *The Bearing of Recent Discovery on the Trustworthiness of the New Testament*, 1915, pp. 376-7, figs. 10-11; A. Deissmann, *Light from the Ancient East*, English ed., 1927, p. 436, figs. 78-9; *SEG*, VI, nos. 558-9; Ramsay, *The Social Basis of Roman Power in Asia Minor*, 1941, pp. 138-9, nos. 145-6.

a) Naiskos with four crescents in field, circle in pediment. Inscription in pediment (first line) and field, so that the crescents are after lines three and four:

Μηνὶ εὐχὴν
Γάμος Ἀβασκάντου
ὑὸς καὶ Λουκᾶς καὶ
Πουμπούμλιος
καὶ Εὔδοξος.

b) Naiskos with one crescent in pediment, three lugged crescents in field. Inscription in pediment, divider, field (crescents before last three lines of inscription):

Μηνὶ
εὐχὴν
Γάμος Ἀβασκάγ[τ-]
ου με(τὰ) γυν[αικὸς],
Λούκιος υἱός,
Πουμπούλιος
υἱός.

196. Hardie, p. 130, no. 18 and fig. 10.
Naiskos with five crescents in field, circle in pediment. Inscription off to left side:

120   CATALOGUE

No. 195

[Φ]αῖδρος
['Α]κάσ[του]
μετὰ τῶ-
ν ἰδίων
Μηνὶ 'Ασ-
καηνῷ
εὐχήν.

197. Hardie, p. 130, no. 19 and fig. 10.
Naiskos with two crescents in field, circle in pediment. To the right, an anepigraphic naiskos with lugged crescent in field. In the field of the main naiskos, under the crescents, the inscription:

Π. 'Αντώνιος
Λ. 'Αντώνιος
Μηνὶ εὐχήν.

198. Hardie, p. 131, no. 20 and fig. 10.
Imitation stele, with one crescent in pediment, five in field. Inscription below:

Μ. Ἔρως μ-
ετὰ τέκνω[ν]
Μηνὶ 'Ασκαην-
ῷ εὐχήν.

199. Hardie, p. 131, no. 21 and fig. 11.
Five naiskoi, side by side, with crescents in field. To the left, anepigraphic naiskos with lugged crescent in field, circle in pediment. Underneath the five:

Κλαύδιος Παῦλος μετὰ τῶν ἰδίων Μηνὶ
'Ασκαηνῷ εὐχήν.

200. Hardie, p. 131, no. 22 and fig. 11.
Three naiskoi, side by side, each with crescent in field, circle in pediment. In the field of the naiskoi, under crescents, respectively:

| 'Αργεία | Demetrius | Ποταμό[ς] |

εὐχήν

Under them all, *LVS* in tabula ansata.

122 CATALOGUE

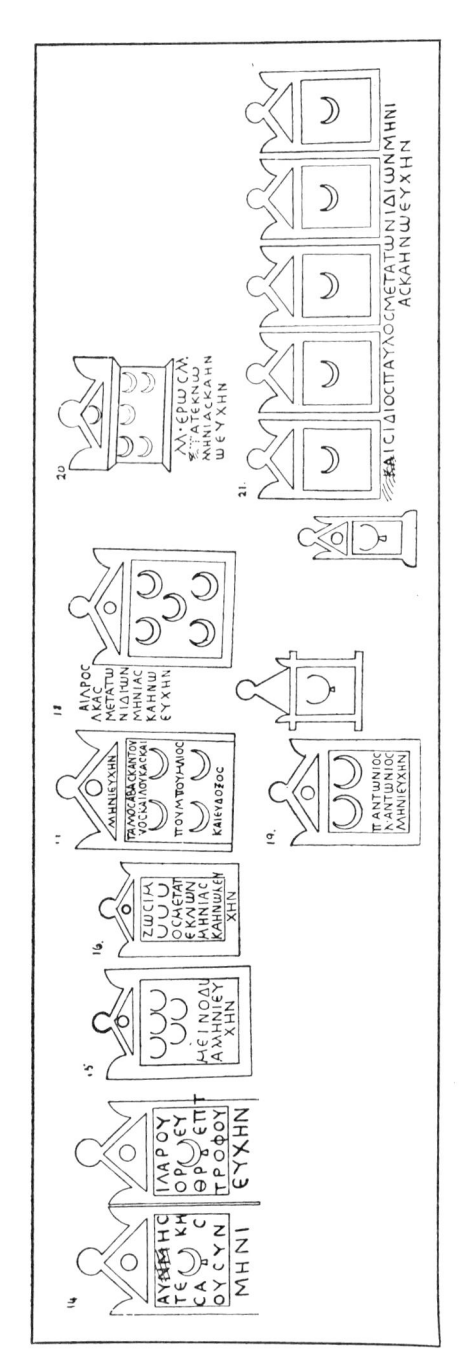

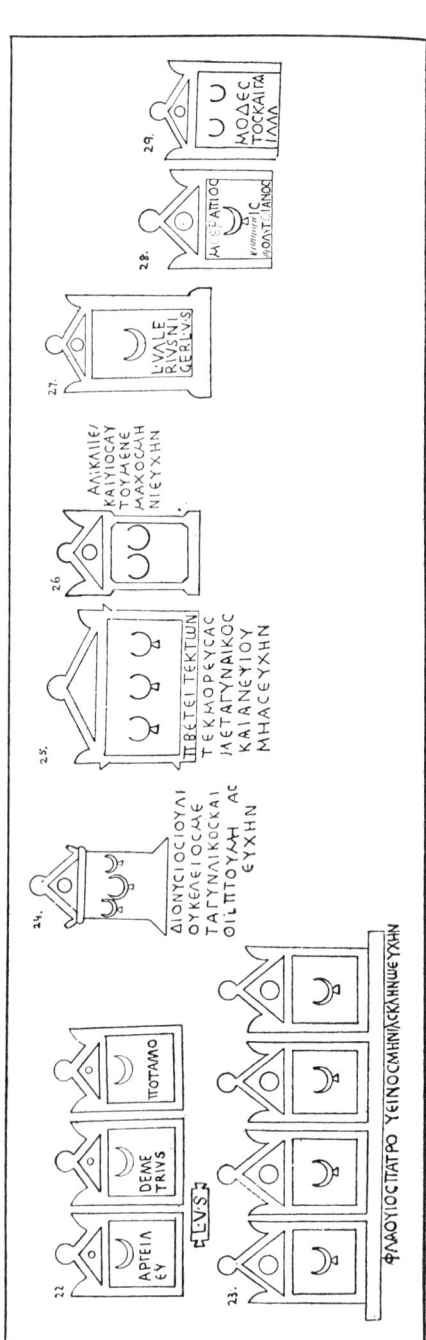

No. 192-207

201. Hardie, p. 131, no. 23 and fig. 11.

Four naiskoi, side by side, each with lugged crescent in field, circle in pediment. A base runs under all four. Underneath is the inscription:

Φλάουιος Πατρούεινος Μηνὶ ᾿Ασκαηνῷ εὐχήν.

202. Hardie, p. 131, no. 24 and fig. 11.

Imitation stele with three lugged crescents in field. Underneath is the inscription:

Διονύσιος ᾿Ιούλι-
ος Κέλερος με-
τὰ γυναικὸς καὶ
θρεπτοῦ Μη[νὶ] ᾿Ασ-
[καηνῷ] εὐχήν.

203. Hardie, p. 131, no. 25 and fig. 11.

Naiskos with three lugged crescents in field. On lower margin and underneath is the following inscription:

Π. Βετεί(λιος) τέκτων
τεκμορεύσας
μετὰ γυναικὸς
καὶ ἀνεψιοῦ
Μη(νὶ) ᾿Ασ(καηνῷ) εὐχήν.

This is the first example we have encountered of the votive formula being abbreviated in the Greek.

204. Hardie, p. 132, no. 26 and fig. 11.

Naiskos with two crescents in field, circle in pediment. Inscription to the right:

[Κ]αλικλῆς
καὶ υἱὸς αὐτ-
οῦ Μενέ-
μαχος Μη-
νὶ εὐχήν.

205. Hardie, p. 132, no. 27 and fig. 11.

Naiskos with crescent in field, circle in pediment. In field under crescent, the inscription:

>L. Vạle-
>rius Ni-
>ger L V S.

206. Hardie, p. 132, no. 28 and fig. 11.

Naiskos with lugged crescent in field, circle in pediment. Inscription in field, one line over crescent, rest under:

>M. Σεράπιος
>..........ις
>· ολ · τριανός

207. Hardie, p. 132, no. 29 and fig. 11.

Naiskos with two crescents in field, circle in pediment. In field under crescent, inscription:

>Μόδεσ-
>τος καὶ Γά-
>ιλλᾳ.

208. Hardie, p. 132, no. 30 and fig. 12.

Imitation stele with one crescent in pediment, three in field. Inscription arranged on entablature, and lower part of field, spilling into right margin, and underneath (top line on entablature, second line on field under crescents, third and fourth underneath):

>Κ. Λόλλιος μετὰ γυναικὸ-
>ς καὶ ἀδελφοῦ καὶ
>θρεπτοῦ τεκμορεύσαν-
>τες Μηνὶ εὐχήν.

209. Hardie, p. 133, no. 31 and fig. 12.

Naiskos with lugged crescent in field, circle in pediment. Naiskos itself has lug at bottom. Inscription in field below crescent:

>M. Ἰούλιος

ASIA MINOR 125

"Ηλιος Μηνὶ
Ἀσκαηνῷ εὐ(χήν).

210. Hardie, p. 133, no. 32 and fig. 12.
Naiskos with three crescents in field, circular ornament in pediment. Inscription underneath:

··· ς Κόιντος
[Λο]ύκιος Τροφί-
[μ]ου Κουίνθου
υἱοὶ Μηνὶ εὐχήν.

211. Hardie, p. 133, no. 33 and fig. 12.
Naiskos with crescent in field. Inscription around crescent, last line underneath:

Μηνὶ Ἀσ-
καηνῷ
εὐχὴν
Κάστωρ
Διονυσί-
ου μετὰ
τῶν ἰδίω-
ν.

212. Hardie, p. 133, no. 34 and fig. 12.
Two naiskoi, one with crescent in field enclosing a rosette, circular ornament in pediment. Written across the field of both, under crescents, the inscription:

Ὑάκινθος Μνησιθέ[ου]
τεκμορεύσας.

Another naiskos to right of last, with three crescents in field, rosette in pediment.

213. Hardie, p. 135, no. 35 and fig. 12.
Naiskos with nine crescents in field, circular ornament in pediment. Underneath, the inscription:

P (?) L V S

126   CATALOGUE

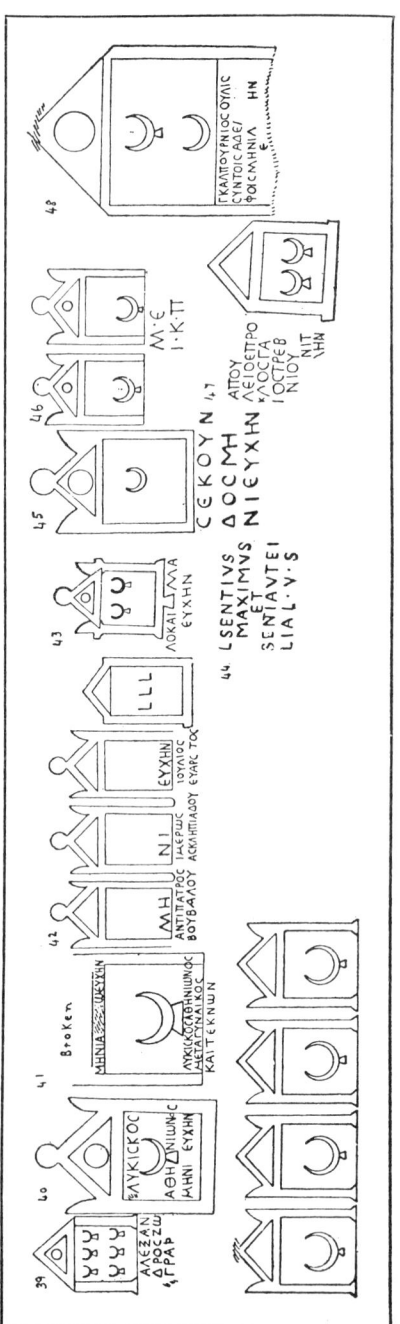

No. 208-224

214. Hardie, p. 135, no. 36 and fig. 12.

Naiskos with two lugged crescents in field, circle in pediment. An appendage at the bottom of the naiskos, as if it were a free standing one. (Cf. nos. 209 and 221. This serves as confirmation for the idea that the crescents with lugs represent free-standing crescents; cf. what I say in Lane, I, about Antioch, no. 42, p. 37). Inscription on bottom margin and underneath:

Κούμητος καὶ
'Ασκάνιος β'
Μηνὶ εὐχήν.

The proper name Askanios is in all probability a deliberate introduction of Roman times. It is perhaps not by accident that a Roman colony was founded at a place where there was a temple of Men Askaenos, and we can reasonably conjecture that the greatest propaganda value possible was derived from this fact. The Romans were made to feel as if this were an ancestral homeland, and the Anatolians, here and at other places in Asia Minor, can be expected to have laid great stress on this title of Men's to emphasize their closeness to the Romans.

215. Hardie, p. 135, no. 37 and fig. 12.

Two naiskoi, each with circle in pediment, four crescents with lugs in the field. Underneath, a tabula ansata with the inscription:

Γάλλος Αὐφούσ-   (perhaps Γάμος)
τιος καὶ Μάρκελλος
Γάιος Οὐείβιος.

216. Hardie, p. 135, no. 38 and fig. 12.

Naiskos with one crescent in field, circle in pediment. Inscription in field around crescent:

Μηνὶ 'Ασκαην-
ῷ εὐχὴν
Γάιος Οὐλτ-
ώνιος Μ-
άξιμος.

217. Hardie, p. 135, no. 39 and fig. 13.

Naiskos with six lugged crescents in field, circle in pediment. Underneath, the inscription:

’Αλέξαν-
δρος ζω-
γράφ[ος].

218. Hardie, p. 135, no. 40 and fig. 13.

Naiskos with lugged crescent in field. Inscription with first line in field over crescent, second two lines under, spilling into right margin:

Λυκίσκος
’Αθηνίωνος
Μηνὶ εὐχήν.

219. Hardie, p. 135, no. 41 and fig. 13.

Naiskos with extremely wide-lugged crescent in field, pediment broken, inscription with first line on entablature, second two in field below crescent, last line underneath:

Μηνὶ ’Α[σκαην]ῷ εὐχὴν
Λυκίσκος ’Αθηνίωνος
μετὰ γυναικὸς
καὶ τέκνων.

Under nos. 218 and 219, there are four anepigraphic naiskoi with lugged crescents in field.

220. Hardie, p. 136, no. 42 and fig. 13.

Four naiskoi without decoration. Across the bottom of the first three:

Μηνὶ εὐχήν.

Below each of the first three:

| ’Αντίπατρος | ‘Ιμέρως | ’Ιούλιος |
| Βουβάλου | ’Ασκληπιάδου | Εὐάρε[σ]τος |

In the field of the fourth, which is on a slightly lower level, and

ASIA MINOR

without the acroteria which characterize the first three: LLL. Probably to be interpreted *libentes*, one L for each dedicator.

221. Hardie, p. 136, no. 43 and fig. 13.
Lugged naiskos with two lugged crescents in field, circle in pediment. Underneath, the inscription:

>Λοκᾶς Μ(ηνὶ) ’Α(σκαηνῷ)
>εὐχήν.

Cf. no. 228 for the abbreviation M.A.

222. Hardie, p. 136, no. 44 and fig. 13.
Inscription alone:

>L. Sentius
>Maximus
>et
>Sentia Utei-
>lia L V S

Cf. no. 179.

223. Hardie, p. 137, no. 45 and fig. 13.
Naiskos with one crescent in field, circle in pediment. Inscription below:

>Σεκοῦν-
>δος Μη-
>νὶ εὐχήν.

224. Hardie, p. 136, no. 46 and fig. 13.
Two naiskoi, each with lugged crescent in field, circle in pediment. Underneath, the inscription:

>M E
>I K Π

The first line is with all probability filled out as:

>Μηνὶ εὐχήν.

The second, conjecturally:

Ἰούλιος καὶ Παῦλος.

225. Hardie, p. 136, no. 47 and fig. 13.
Naiskos with two lugged crescents in field. Inscription to left side, damaged:

Ἀπου-
λεῖος Πρό-
κλος Γά-
ιος Τρεβ-
[ω]νίου
· · · · νιτ
· · · · Μην[ὶ].

226. Hardie, p. 136, no. 48 and fig. 13.
Naiskos with two crescents in field, upper one with lug, lower one without; circle in pediment. Under the crescents, the following inscription:

Γ. Καλπούρνιος Οὖλις
σὺν τοῖς ἀδελ-
φοῖς Μηνὶ Ἀ[σκα]ην[ῷ]
ε[ὐχήν].

227. Hardie, p. 138, nos. 49 and 50, and fig. 14.
Three anepigraphic naiskoi, each of which has a crescent in field. Below the one to the right, a fourth similar naiskos. Around the top of it, the inscription:

Li(bens) M(erito)
G. Valer(ius)
cum s[u-]
is fili-
is L V
S

228. Hardie, p. 139, no. 51 and fig. 14.

ASIA MINOR

131

Two naiskoi (or imitation steles?). The one to the left has one crescent in pediment, three in field. The one to the right has two crescents in pediment, three in field. To the right there is perhaps an erased area. Inscription below naiskoi:

Μάντοι Λούκιος καὶ Μᾶρκος τεκμορεύσαντες
μετὰ γυναικῶν καὶ τέκνων M. A.

This is the second example we have had of the abbreviation M.A. It is to be interpreted Μηνὶ Ἀσκαηνῷ. Cf. no. 203 and 221.

229. Hardie, p. 139, no. 52 and fig. 14.
Two naiskoi, each with lugged crescent in field. Below, the inscription:

····νεος υἱὸς Διονυσίο[υ] Μηνὶ εὐχὴν
σὺν θυγατρί μ[ο]υ Ἰσ[μ]άρῃ.

230. Hardie, p. 139, no. 53 and fig. 14.
Not *in situ*, but on a block found in a church near the site of the temple of Men. Naiskos with two lugged crescents in field, circle in pediment. In field below crescents, the inscription:

Πούβλιος
μετὰ γυναι-
κὸς Μηνὶ
εὐχήν.

231. Hardie, p. 139, no. 54 and fig. 14.
Two naiskoi, each with crescent in field. Inscriptions in field of each one under crescents (Hardie's interpretation):

a) G(aiae) l(ibertus)	b) G(aiae) l(ibertus) Iulius
Alexander	Belus
L V S	L V S

232. Hardie, p. 139, no. 55 and fig. 14.
Naiskos with two lugged crescents, one in pediment, one in field.

132 CATALOGUE

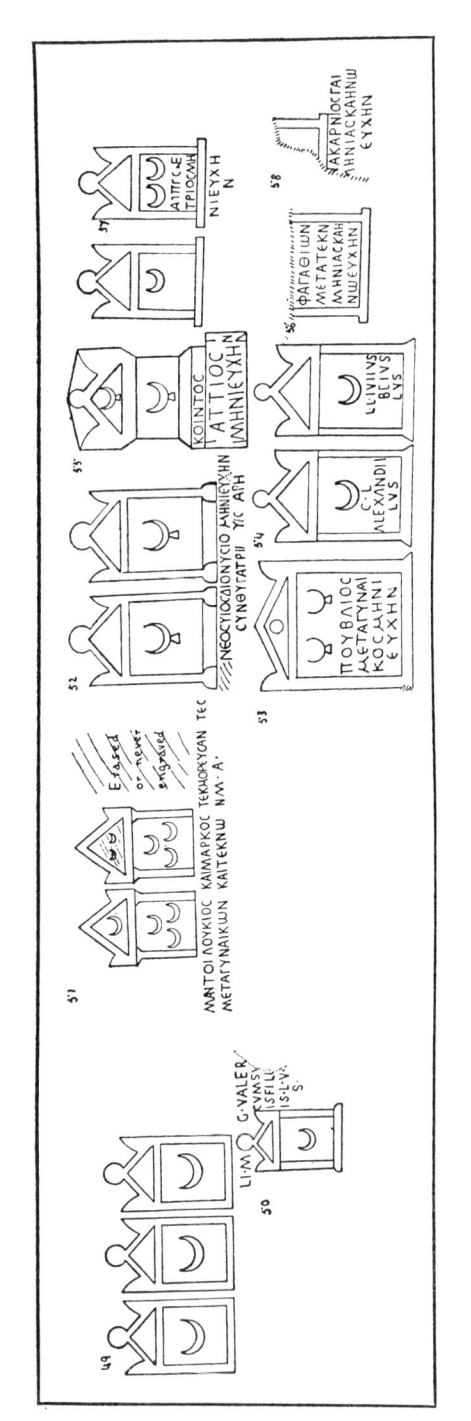

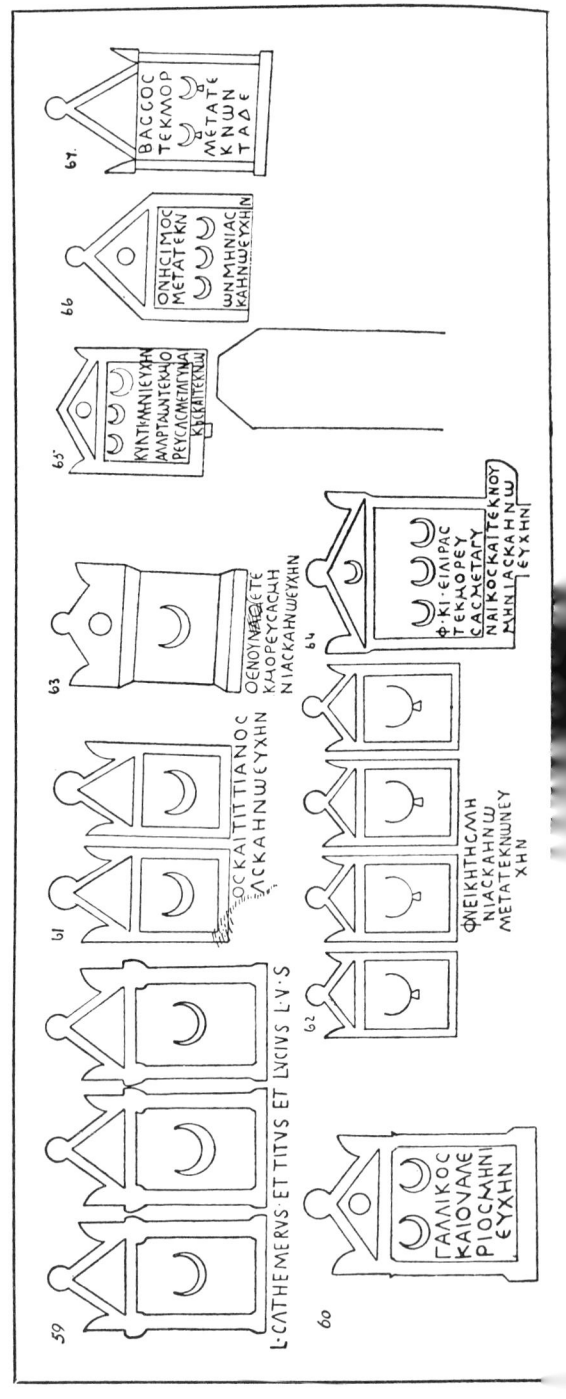

On lower margin and below, the inscription:

Κόιντος
Ἄττιος
Μηνὶ εὐχήν.

233. Hardie, p. 140, no. 56 and fig. 14.
Bottom of a naiskos with no crescent preserved. Inscription in field:

Φ. Ἀγαθίων
μετὰ τέκ(νων)
Μηνὶ Ἀσκαη-
νῷ εὐχήν.

234. Hardie, p. 140, no. 57 and fig. 14.
Two naiskoi, one to left with one crescent in field, one to right with two in field. In field of and below one to right, the inscription:

Ἄππως Νέ-
τριος Μη-
νὶ εὐχήν.

235. Hardie, p. 140, no. 58 and fig. 14.
Lower right corner of a naiskos without preserved decoration. Below:

[Ο]ὐακάρνιος Γάι-
[ος] Μηνὶ Ἀσκαηνῷ
εὐχήν.

236. Hardie, p. 141, no. 59 and fig. 15.
Three naiskoi, each with crescent in field. Underneath the three:

L. Cathemerus et Titus et Lucius L V S.

237. Hardie, p. 141, no. 60 and fig. 15.
Naiskos with two crescents in field, circle in pediment. In field, under the crescents:

Γαλλικὸς
καὶ Οὐαλέ-
ριος Μηνὶ
εὐχήν.

238. Hardie, p. 141, no. 61 and fig. 15.
Two naiskoi, each with crescent in field. Underneath, the inscription:

·····ος καὶ Τιττιανὸς
[Μηνὶ] ᾿Ασκαηνῷ εὐχήν.

239. Hardie, p. 141, no. 62 and fig. 15.
Four naiskoi, each with lugged crescent in field. Underneath, the inscription:

Φ. Νεικήτης Μη-
νὶ ᾿Ασκαηνῷ
μετὰ τέκνων εὐ-
χήν.

240. Hardie, p. 141, no. 63 and fig. 15.
Naiskos (or imitation stele?) with one crescent in field, circle in pediment. Underneath, the inscription:

᾿Οενούαος τε-
κμορεύσας Μη-
νὶ ᾿Ασκαηνῷ εὐχήν.

241. Hardie, p. 141, no. 64 and fig. 15.
Naiskos with one crescent in pediment, three in field. Perhaps intended as having lug at bottom. In field under crescents and on lower margin, the inscription:

Φ. Κί(γκιος) Εἰλάρας
τεκμορεύ-
σας μετὰ γυ-
ναικὸς καὶ τέκνου
Μηνὶ ᾿Ασκαηνῷ
εὐχήν.

242. Hardie, p. 141, no. 65 and fig. 15.

Naiskos, perhaps intended as having lug at bottom, having three crescents of increasing size left to right in field, circle in pediment. Inscription under crescents, and in lower and right margins:

> Κύγτις Μηνὶ εὐχὴν
> ἁμαρτάγων τεκμο-
> ρεύσας μετὰ γυναι-
> κὸς καὶ τέκνων.

Here, if the reading is correct (ἁμαρτάνων is sloppily written, with ligatures), the action of τεκμορεύειν is taken as an expiation for sin. Cf. my no. 77, from Sardis.

243. Hardie, p. 142, no. 66 and fig. 15.

Naiskos with three crescents in field, circle in pediment. Inscription in field and on right margin, two lines over crescents and two lines under:

> Ὀνήσιμος
> μετὰ τέκν-
> ων Μηνὶ Ἀσ-
> καηνῷ εὐχήν.

244. Hardie, p. 142, no. 67 and fig. 15.

Naiskos with two lugged crescents in field. Inscription in field, two lines over crescents, two lines under:

> Βάσσος
> τεκμορ[εύσας]
> μετὰ τέ-
> κνων
> τάδε.

So far we have dealt mainly with inscriptions on the walls of the temple enclosure. The following are free-standing and may have been inserted into niches on the wall:

245. Hardie, p. 143, no. 68 and fig. 16.

A marble tablet of naiskos shape, with elaborate decoration, including three crescents in pediment, seven across the divider between pediment and field. Present whereabouts unknown. In field, the inscription:

Λ. Ἀντιόχου καὶ
Ἀντίοχος ἀδελφὸς
καὶ Μαξίμα ἀδελφὴ
μετὰ τέκνων καὶ
θρεπτῶν τεκμο-
ρεύσαντες Μηνὶ
Ἀσκαηνῷ εὐχήν.

No. 245

246. Hardie, p. 143, no. 69 and fig. 17.
A fragment of a tablet similar to no. 245. Inscription:

. . . . σ
. . . . τερμορ-
[εύσαντες Μηνὶ Ἀσ]κηνῷ.

ASIA MINOR 137

Nos. 246-247

247. Hardie, p. 143, no. 70 and fig. 18.
A fragment similar to no. 246. Inscription:

Κείπιος Ἀσπρίνας
[τε]κμορεύσας μετὰ
[γυ]ναικὸς Μηνὶ εὐχήν.

248. Two naiskoi, likewise in wall of temple enclosure. Each has a crescent. Inscription in field below crescents, and below the left naiskos.
Dimensions unknown.
   Bibliography: Ramsay, *Bearing*, p. 374, fig. 9; Lane, II, p. 47.
Inscription:

a) in field of left naiskos

Λουκᾶς
Τίλλιο-
ς Κρίτω-
ν

No. 248

b) in field of right naiskos

Νουμε-
ρία Οὐε-
νοῦστ-
α

c) below left naiskos

Μηνὶ
εὐχήν.

249. A marble stele with pediment, acroteria, and circular ornament in center. Known at least since 1924. There is an ornament in the field as if the ends of a wreath had been pulled together and tied in a knot. Within wreath there is a crescent. Inscription is below ornament. Now in Konya Museum.

Dimensions: Height 41 cm., width 30 cm., thickness 5.5 cm.

Bibliography: Ramsay, *Social Basis*, p. 143, no. 149; Lane, II, p. 47.

Inscription:

M. Albucius Firmus
L V S

250. A fragmentary stele with ornament likely to be restored as a wreath. Known at least since 1924. Inscription below ornament, last line on raised surface at base. Now in Konya Museum.

Dimensions: Maximum width 23 cm., preserved height 17 cm.

    Bibliography: Ramsay, *Social Basis*, p. 143, no. 150; Lane, II, p. 47.

Inscription:

            C. Albucius
            Firmus L V S L M

(If LM means Libens Merito, this is further argument against LVS meaning Libens Votum Solvit. Why say it twice?) Cf. no. 227.

Cf. the argument in Lane I, p. 30, and Levick, *AS*, XX, 1970, pp. 49-50.

251. A dedication mentioned by Ramsay without description or even full text.

Dimensions unknown.

    Bibliography: Ramsay, *Social Basis*, p. 23, no. 10; Lane, II, p. 47.

Inscription contains name:

            M. Ulpius
            Pudens
            Pompeianus

252. A rock-cut inscription in a "small rock sanctuary" near Yalvaç. Known since 1916. The inscription is in a tabula ansata.

Dimensions: Length 75 cm., height 25 cm., letters 2.5 cm.

    Bibliography: Pace, *Annuario*, III, 1916-20, pp. 57-58, no. 51; *SEG*, II, 1925, no. 750; Lane, II, p. 47.

The inscription reads:

        [Οὐ]είβιος Φίρμος Καπίτων μετὰ
        [γυ]ναικὸς καὶ τέκνων τεκ[μ]ορεύσας
        Μηνὶ Ἀσκαηνῷ εὐχήν.

253. A tabula ansata of marble, broken slightly on the left. Known since 1967. It is surrounded by a border. At the top of the field, there are three crescents, of which the middle one is surrounded by a wreath. Inscription under crescents. Now in Yalvaç Museum.

Dimensions: Width 31 cm., height 25 cm., thickness 2.5 cm.

Bibliography: B. Levick, *AS*, XVII, 1967, p. 117, no. 46; L. Robert, *REG*, LXXXI, 1968, p. 529, no. 540; Lane, II, p. 47.

The inscription reads:

Μ. Σενπρώνιος Κάρπος
τεκμορεύσας μετὰ τέκνων
Μηνὶ Ἀσκαηνῷ εὐχὴν δ'.

254. Fragment from lower right hand corner of stele. The preserved portion of the stele contains the lower portion of a pilaster, which must have been repeated on the left side. Under the pilasters there was a tabula ansata. In 1967, in Yalvaç Library.

Preserved dimensions: Width 22 cm., height 28.5 cm., thickness 4 cm.

Bibliography: Levick, *op. cit.*, p. 118, no. 47 and Pl. XIIIa; Robert, *loc. cit.*; Lane, II, p. 47.

The inscriptions had the first four lines between the pilasters, the last four on the tabula ansata. It reads:

[Γ. Φλάουιο]ς Λόν-
[γος τεκμο]ρεύ-
[σας μετ]ὰ γυ-
[ναικὸς] ❦
[· · · · · · · καὶ υἱῶ]ν Γ. Φλαου-
[ίου Λόνγου καὶ] Φλαουίου
[· · · · · · · · · · Μηνὶ] Ἀσκαινῷ
[εὐχήν.]

255. A large stone first seen by Barbara Levick in use as part of a stairway in a house in Yalvaç in 1967 or earlier, transported thence to the courtyard of the Yalvaç Museum, where it was in 1969.

Dimensions: Length 1.02 m., width 51 cm., thickness irregular.

The stone bears the inscription:

Ἡ τράπεζα Μηνός,
Πρωτίωνος εὐχή.

It will be treated at length in a forthcoming article by Miss Barbara Levick.

256. A "broken dedication" to Men from the sanctuary. Published by Ramsay without adequate description.
Dimensions unknown.
>Bibliography: Ramsay, *JRS*, VIII, 1918, p. 118; Lane, I, p. 39, note 143.

The inscription reads:

>>M. Cl. Clito-
>>machus et
>>Cornelia An-
>>tonis uxor eius
>>L V S
>>L   V   [S]

257. Another dedication from the sanctuary, published by Ramsay without adequate description.
Dimensions unknown.
>Bibliography: Ramsay, *loc. cit.*; Lane, *loc. cit.*

The inscription reads:

>>M. Cl. Clitomachus cum
>>fil(iis) Cl. Prisco et Tauro
>>L   V   S

258. Another dedication, fallen from S.W. wall of sanctuary. Published by Ramsay without adequate description.
Dimensions unknown.
>Bibliography: Ramsay, *op. cit.*, p. 133; Lane, *loc. cit.*

The inscription, as interpreted by Ramsay, reads:

>>Ἰόν(ιος) κατ(ὰ) τελ(ετὴν)
>>μετ(ὰ) τέκ(νων)
>>Μην(ὶ) Ἀσκ(αηνῷ) εὐχ(ήν).

259. A stele of honey-colored marble broken at top, lug at bottom, now in the Wilson Collection of the University of Aberdeen. Reportedly from Pisidian Antioch, perhaps found in the excavations. Unpublished.

Dimensions: Height 13.5 cm., width 19.3 cm., thickness 4 cm., letters 1.5 cm., interlineation .5 cm.

The stele bears the following inscription:

. . . .
τεκμορεύσας
σὺν γυναικὶ
Μηνὶ Ἀσκαηνῷ
εὐχήν.

260. A plaque of marble, ostensibly found by D. M. Robinson in the excavations carried out in 1924 on the site of the forum of Antioch, now in Konya Archaeological Museum.

Dimensions: Height 49 cm., width 35 cm., thickness 9 cm.

Bibliography: Lane, I, p. 36, no. 37 and Plate V, no. 1.

The plaque is in the form of a naiskos with acroteria, showing a bust of Men in an arched recess. Men wears a Phrygian cap, and there is a crescent behind and on either side of his head. The bust in relief would seem to be an imitation of a bust in the round, for it is portrayed with a little base to stand on. Inscription below, in scratchy writing:

Γαῖος Γαίου τοῦ Λουκίου
τεκμορεύσας σὺν καὶ
Πανκάρπῳ θρεπτῷ
ἰδίῳ Μηνὶ Ἀσκαηνῷ
εὐχήν.

For this and the following inscriptions, see now Addenda.

261. A plaque of marble, found at same time and housed in same place as above.

Dimensions: Height 60 cm., width 39 cm., thickness 6 cm.

Bibliography: Lane, I, p. 37, no. 38 and Pl. V, no. 2.

The plaque is in the form of a naiskos with pediment and acroteria. On either side of the main field, there is an anta. Under the pediment there is an egg-and-dart moulding. In the middle of the pediment is a circular ornament. In the main field there is a wreath with a circular ornament at the top, a ribbon at the bottom. Within the wreath there are two crescents side by side, and one crescent each in each of the top corners of the field. Each crescent is split down the middle lengthwise by a line of unknown significance. Under the wreath is the following inscription:

>Q. Licinius Naevius
>f. et Aurelia Procula uxor
>eius et Aureli Proculus et
>C. et L. M. f.
>L V S

The last line is on the margin under the field.

262. Two fragments of a marble plaque, found at same time and housed in same place as above.
Dimensions: (as restored) Height 37 cm., width 22.5 cm.
Bibliography: Lane, I, p. 37, no. 39, and Pl. V, no. 3.

The plaque was in the form of a stele, with a pediment topped by a vegetative decoration. On either side of the main field was an anta likewise containing a vegetative motif. In the middle of the pediment there was a circular ornament, and in the middle of the main field a recessed medallion with a bust of Men, with crescent at shoulders, wearing Phrygian cap. On the margin under the main field is the following inscription:

>Γ. Σερουείλιος Μύρτιλος
>τεκμορεύσας γ' Μηνὶ 'Ασκαηνῷ εὐχήν.

263. Marble plaque of which three fragments are preserved, found at same time and housed in same place as above.
Dimensions: (as the pieces are fitted together in plaster in the museum) Height 37 cm., width 25 cm., thickness 4 cm.
Bibliography: Lane, I, p. 37, no. 41 and Pl. V, no. 4.

The only decoration preserved on the plaque is the bottom of an anta on the left side. There is also part of the top margin, as well as most of the bottom margin, preserved. The plaque bears the following inscription (conjectural restorations furnished by Miss Barbara Levick):

[Γ.] Οὐέττιο[ς ····]
[···]κ(αὶ) Τ. Οὐέτ[τιος]
[Κα]πίτων Ν[έος]
[κ(αὶ)] Παῦλα κ(αὶ) [····]
[···] Μαξίμα [ἀδελ-]
φοὶ σὺν [·········]
τι κ(αὶ) Πρε[ίσκῳ θρε-]
πτοῖς τ[εκμορεύ-]
σαντες [Μηνὶ Θεῷ]
🌙 πατ[ρίῳ] 🌙
εὐχή[ν].

264. Roughly square marble slab of which eight pieces are preserved, found at same time and housed in same place as above.
Dimensions: Height 38 cm., width 40 cm., thickness 4 cm.
Bibliography: Lane, I, p. 37, no. 42 and Pl. VI, no. 1.

The plaque bears relief representations of three crescents, arranged in a V. Each crescent has a lug at the bottom, and would thus seem to be a representation of a free-standing crescent that could be set in a base. It also bears the following inscription, of which the first two lines are interrupted by the lowest crescent, the remaining lines being below the crescents:

Εὐδαίμων Γνωστοῦ
υἱὸς
τεκμορεύσας μετὰ τῶν ἰδίων
θρεπτῶν Μηνὶ Ἀσκαηνῷ
τὸ β΄ εὐχήν.

265. Similar slab of which five pieces are preserved, found at same time and housed in same place as preceding.
Dimensions: Height 34 cm., width 32 cm., thickness 4 cm.
Bibliography: Lane, I, p. 38, no. 43 and Pl. VI, no. 2.

The stone has no decoration outside of a border. It bears the following inscription:

[····]υμο[····]
[····]οικκ[···]

Φρούγει
τεκμορεύσας
Μηνὶ εὐχήν.

266. Stele similar to number 262. Also reportedly from the 1924 excavations of Antioch. Seen by the author in 1961 in a storeroom of the Selcuk Museum (Ince Minare) of Konya, but not transferred to display in the Archaeological Museum, like its counterparts.
Dimensions unavailable.

Bibliography: Lane, I, p. 37, no. 40.

The stele portrayed a circular ornament in the pediment and in the main field three crescents in a wreath. Underneath, the inscription:

Μάξιμος Λουκίου τεκμορεύσας μετὰ τῶν ἰδίων Μηνὶ πατ(ρίῳ) εὐχήν.

(I am omitting from consideration the items numbered Lane, I, p. 38, nos. 44 and 46-50. These were all seen by the author at the same time and place as no. 266, but are all so fragmentary or inconclusive as not to be of great importance. I have also been able to acquire no further information on most of them, other than what I acquired on my fleeting visit.)

267. Pedimental stele presumably found at same time and in same place as preceding. Now in Archaeological Museum of Konya.
Dimensions: Height 38 cm., width 23 cm., thickness 5 cm.

The stele has non-vegetative acroteria and, in the center, a crescent moon with appendages at ends. In the main field there is a representation of a wreath tied with a ribbon. The surface of the bottom part is heavily damaged.
Inscription:

a) on entablature

Τειμόθεος Ἀλεξάνδρου

b) on bottom

. . . . ν
Μ[ηνὶ Ἀσκαηνῷ εὐχ]ήν.

268. Pedimental stele with lug found at same time and place as foregoing, now in same place.

Dimensions: Height 72 cm., width 30 cm., thickness 12.5 cm.

The stele has vegetative acroteria and a flower (or star?) within a deep center recess. In the main field, between antae, is a bust of Men with crescent and Phrygian cap. At the bottom is the inscription:

Εὔβουλος Σωσίου
ὑπὲρ ἑαυτοῦ καὶ τέκνων
Μ(ηνὶ) Ἀ(σκαηνῷ) ε(ὐχήν).

269. An epigraphical stele, found at same time and in same place as preceding, now in same museum.

Dimensions: Height 41 cm., width 24 cm., thickness 9 cm.

The stele (actually squared at the top), has non-vegetative acroteria in relief, and a star on either side of the central acroterion. In the pediment, there is one lugged crescent with appendages, and in the main field six such crescents. Although the name of the god nowhere appears on this stone, the association with his cult is evident.

270. Votive altar, found at same time and place as foregoing., now in same museum.

Dimensions: Height 40.5 cm., width 19 cm., thickness 17 cm.

At the top of the main field there are three crescents. Under them there is the following inscription, of which the last line is on the base:

Ἀσκληπιάδης
Πρείμου
μετὰ καὶ τῶν
υἱῶν Ἀσκλη-
πιάδου καὶ Κο-
ίντου τεκμο-
ρεύσας Μηνὶ
Πατρίῳ εὐχήν.

271. Three fragments of a marble plaque found at same time and place as foregoing, now in same museum.

Dimensions: Preserved height 24.5 cm., width as restored in plaster, 26.5 cm.

Bibliography: Lane, I, p. 38, no. 45.

The fragment has traces of a pediment, columns, and a wreath on the main field. Under the wreath is the following inscription:

Λ. Λόλ[λιο]ς Πρεῖσ-
κος τ[εκμορε]ύσας

272. Two fragments from bottom of marble plaque with frame around it, found at same time and place as above and now in same museum.

Dimensions: Preserved height 11 cm., preserved width 22 cm.

The following inscription can be read in the main field:

τ· · · · · · · · · · · · · · ·
τρ· · · · · · · · · · · · ·
on base   τεκ[μ]ορεύσα[· · · · ·]

273. Two fragments of a plaque of marble, found at same time and same place as foregoing and now in same museum.

Dimensions: Preserved height 18 cm., preserved width 18 cm.

The following inscription can be read, with lines drawn under the letters. The last line of the inscription is on the base, the remainder on the main field:

[· · · ·] Γ. Νεικάνορο[ς καὶ]
[Νει]κάνωρ Ἀλεξάν[δρου]
[σὺ]ν τοῖς ἰδίοις [καὶ]
[θρε]πτοῖς τεκμορε[ύσαντες]
[Μην]ὶ Ἀσκαηνῷ [εὐχήν.]

274. Two fragments of a lugged stele found in the same place and at same time as foregoing, now in same museum.

Dimensions: Preserved height 15.5 cm., width 19.5 cm.

In the main field, between antae, the following inscription can be read:

....
Ζωτ[ικὸς μετὰ ····]
τος καὶ Εὐτύχι-
δος ἰδίων τε-
κμορεύσας
Μηνὶ Ἀσκαηνῷ
εὐχήν.

275. Three fragments of a plaque of marble, found at the same time and place as foregoing, now in same museum.

Dimensions: Preserved height 13 cm., preserved width 14.5 cm.

In the main field, under a fragment of a representation in relief, the following inscription can be made out:

[······]τιος Ἀνιη[···]
[······] Τρίτος [·····]
[τεκμορ]εύσας Μη[νὶ]
[Ἀσκαην]ῷ εὐχήν.

276. Three fragments of a tabula ansata of marble, found at the same time and place as foregoing, now in same museum.

Dimensions: Height 26.5 cm., preserved width 22 cm.

In the main field the following inscription can be made out:

[Μηνὶ ε]ὐχήν
....
....
[······]ορος
[Μακ]εδών.

277. Three fragments of a marble plaque, found at the same time and place as foregoing, now in same museum.

Dimensions: Preserved height 14 cm., preserved width 21 cm.

There are the remains of a representation of a crescent with a ribbon at either side. Under the relief, the following inscription can be read:

[·····]πορος μετὰ τέκνων[·····]
[·····]ος, Δόκιμος μετὰ γυ[ναικὸς]
[·····]μνόη καὶ Μαρ[········]

278. Three fragments of tabula ansata of marble, found in same place at same time as foregoing, now in same museum.

Dimensions: Height 24.5 cm., preserved width 24 cm.

In the top center of the main field there are traces of a representation of a crescent. The following inscription can be read, of which the first line is on the top margin, the last on the bottom margin, and the rest in the field under the crescent:

Ἀγαθῇ [Τύχῃ]
Θεοδο[·····]
Ποσειδ[·····]
Ἑρμογα[····]
Τροφον[·····]
Ἀσκαηνῷ [εὐχήν].

279. Five fragments of a lugged stele found at the same place and same time as foregoing, now in same museum.

Dimensions: Preserved height 18 cm., width 20 cm.

At the top of the preserved portion there is a crescent in relief. Under it there is the following inscription, of which the last three lines are on the bottom margin:

Τίτος Οὐίσενν-
ος Μάξιμος τε-
κμορεύσας μετὰ
γυνα[ι]κὸς καὶ τέ-
κνου Τίτου Οὐισέν[ν-]
ου Μαξί-
μου.

280. Three fragments of a stele found in the same place and at the same time as the the foregoing, now in same museum.

Dimensions: Preserved height 17.5 cm., width 33 cm.

The stele had the representation, between antae, of a bull facing left. Under the relief field, in and on the bottom margin of a tabula, is the following inscription:

Γ. Καλπούρνιος Ζώ[σι]μος καὶ Γ. Καλπούρνιος Ζωτικὸς τεκμορεύσαντες
Μηνὶ ἐπηκόῳ εὐχήν.

281. Four fragments of a marble plaque, found at the same time and same place as preceding, now in same museum.

Dimensions: Preserved height 22 cm., preserved width 23 cm.

The plaque had a raised margin running around it. At the top of the field there are visible four crescents, and under them the following inscription:

[· · · ·]Τειμόθ[εος]
[μετ]ὰ γυναικὸς
[καὶ τέκν]ων τε[κμορεύσας]
[Μηνὶ ’Α]σκ[αηνῷ]
[εὐχήν.]

282. Four fragments of a stele of marble found in the same place at the same time as foregoing, now in same museum.

Dimensions: Preserved height 25 cm., width 28 cm.

The stele has a representation in relief of a bust of Men with crescent and Phrygian cap within a wreath tied by ribbons at the bottom. In the field under the wreath ribbons and on the bottom margin is the following inscription:

Λουκι[· · · · · · · · ·]ος
[· · · ·]ν[· · · · · · · · ·]ωτικῷ σύν

(Unless we have σύν used postpositively, this is an odd way for the inscription to end, but there does not appear to have been anything following.)

283. Four fragments of a marble tablet found in the same place and at the same time as foregoing, now in same museum.

Dimensions: Preserved height 20 cm., preserved width 26.5 cm.

The stone bears the representation of a wreath with ribbons tied at the bottom. To the sides and under the wreath is the following inscription:

    μβρ   σκοπτο
    τωλης μετὰ γυ-
    ναικὸς τεκμο-
    [ρεύ]σας Μηνὶ
    ['Α]σκαηνῷ εὐχήν.

284. Three fragments of a marble stele, found in the same place and at same time as foregoing, now in same museum.

Dimensions: Preserved height 22 cm., width 30 cm.

The stone bears traces of a crescent in relief. Under the relief, between two antae, is the following inscription:

    [Τιβ]έριος Κλ(α)ύδι-
    ος Φρούγει τεκ-
    μορεύσας Μη-
    νὶ εὐχήν.

285. Four fragments of a marble plaque, found at the same time and same place as preceding, now in same museum.

Dimensions: Preserved height 18 cm., preserved width 25 cm.

The stone bears a representation of three crescents with lugs and appendages on the tips. Above the crescents, very faintly, can be read the inscription:

    Μηνὶ ἐπ[η]κόῳ

Under the crescents can be read:

    ευιοισυμφ
    [Τ]ρόφιμος Μακε[δών].

286. Four fragments of a marble plaque, found at the same time and in same place as foregoing, now in same museum.

Dimensions: Preserved height 22 cm., preserved width 25 cm.

The stone was originally surrounded by a raised margin. There was no relief, but the field contains the following inscription:

>   Λυτρόνιος
>   Μαρχε[ιαν]ός
>   [Μ]ηνὶ 'Ασκα[ηνῷ]
>   εὐχ[ήν].

287. Six fragments of a stele with a lug at the bottom, found at the same time and same place as the foregoing, now in same museum.

Dimensions: Preserved height 43.5 cm., preserved width 30 cm.

The stele bears a decoration containing two antae supporting an entablature. In the main field, there is an elaborate wreath, with ribbons tied at the bottom, enclosing a crescent. Over the wreath there are three crescents, and there is one crescent at each of the lower corners.

The stone bears the following inscription, of which the first line is on the entablature, the last on the lower margin, the remainder in the main field under the wreath:

>   [····]ούλιος Ταρε[·····]
>   τεκμορεύσα[ς]
>   μετὰ γυναικ[ὸς]
>   καὶ τέκνων κ[αὶ]
>   θρεπτῶν Μην[ὶ]
>   'Ασκαηνῷ [εὐχήν].

288. Nine fragments of a marble plaque, found at the same time and place as foregoing, now in same museum.

Dimensions: Height 41 cm., preserved width 43 cm.

The plaque has a representation at the bottom of a bull facing left, behind him a flaming altar. Above, there is a tabula, at the top of which there is a row of crescents, of which five are visible. Under the crescents there is the following inscription:

[· · · ·]υνήτιος Πωλι-
[· · · ·] Αὐξάνων με-
[τὰ γυ]ναικὸς Μαρκίας καὶ
τέ[κν]ων καὶ θρεπτοῦ
Μηνὶ Πατρίῳ εὐχήν.

289. Four fragments of a stele of marble, found at the same time and same place as foregoing, now in same museum.

Dimensions: Height 35 cm., width 27.5 cm.

The stone bears a design of two columns supporting an architrave. In the top of the field there is a medallion, probably once containing a bust of Men; under the medallion is the following inscription:

Οὐετ[τί]α
Μαγνίλλα ☽
τεκμορεύσασς
Μηνὶ Ἀσκαηνῷ
εὐχήν.

290. Three fragments of a tabula ansata, found at the same time and in the same place as foregoing, now in same museum.

Dimensions: Height 34.5 cm., preserved width 31 cm.

The tabula ansata is surrounded by a raised margin. At the top there is a row of four crescents, and under them the following inscription:

Τ. Κλαύδιος Πασι-
νιανὸς Νέος Σουμ-
μαρούδης τεκμο-
ρεύσας μετὰ γυναι-
κὸς καὶ ἀδελφῶν
Μηνὶ Πατρί[ῳ]
εὐχήν.

291. Two fragments of a lugged stele found at the same time and place as foregoing, now in same museum.

Dimensions: Preserved height 28 cm., width 24 cm.

The stele bears, between antae, a representation of a wreath tied with ribbons at the bottom. Within the wreath is a crescent. There is also the following inscription, of which the first two lines are above the wreath, the next two in the field under the wreath, and the last on the bottom margin:

    Γ. ʹΗούλειος Μᾶρκος
    καὶ Μάρ   κελλος
    ἀδελφοὶ
    τεκμορεύσαντες μετὰ
    θρεπτοῦ Μηνὶ ʹΑσκαηνῷ εὐχήν.

292. Three fragments of a marble plaque, found at the same time and place as foregoing, now in same museum.

Dimensions: Preserved height 18 cm., width as restored in plaster 34 cm.

The plaque had a raised margin running around it. There is no preserved indication of a relief, but there is an inscription in writing singularly full of ligatures:

    [· · · · · · · · ·]ωνος
    [· · · · · · · · ·]ας
    [· · · · · · · · ·] τεκμο-
    [ρ]εύσας Μ[ηνὶ ʹΑσ]καηνῷ
    εὐ[χήν].

293. Two fragments of a marble stele, found at the same time and place as foregoing, now in same museum.

Dimensions: Preserved height 21 cm., preserved width 18 cm.

The stele bears a decoration of two antae supporting an entablature. At the top of the main field there is a wreath surrounding a crescent. On the entablature there is the inscription:

    [καὶ τ]έκνου Μηνο[· · · · · ·]

Under the relief there is the inscription:

Π. Κλαύδιος [······]
τεκμορεύσα[ς μετὰ]
Μαρίας Γαία[ς γυναι-]
κὸς
Μη[νὶ 'Ασκαηνῷ εὐχήν.]

The last line is on the lower margin.

294. Fragment of stele, found at the same time and place as foregoing. Seen by Barbara Levick in Konya in 1955, but not now on display in the museum.

Dimensions: Preserved height 22.5 cm., preserved width 27 cm.

The stone bears a portion of an anta on the right, and in the field the inscription:

[····]ώνιος
[····]είου υἱὸς
[τεχ]μορεύσας
[Μη]νὶ 'Ασκαηνῷ
εὐχήν.

DUBIA

Here among the dubia I propose to include only those items, which, while their connection with Men is far from definite, still possess in my estimation some likelihood of being connected with the cult. Items whose connection with Men either is very far-fetched, or has been conclusively disproved, I deliberately exclude: e.g., the Sounion inscriptions, *IG*, II², 2937 and 2940 (cf., Lane, I, p. 6, note 3); the Konya inscription, *CIG*, 4000 (cf. Lane, I, p. 47, note 173).

Athenae: Athens, Greece

D1. A bronze plaque, broken in three pieces, found in the Agora Excavations, March 18, 1937. Now in the Agora Museum.
Dimensions: Height 23.5 cm., maximum width 14.4 cm.

Bibliography: Lane, I, p. 9, no. 11 and Plate II, no. 2.

The plaque has a boundary of a stylized leaf-pattern, which also separates the pediment from the main field of the aedicula. At the top and each corner of the pediment there are floral acroteria, that on the right now being broken. There is a 7-rayed star in each interior corner of the pediment. In the center of the pediment there is a circle containing a frontal bust (Men?) on a large crescent. At the bottom of the preserved portion of the main field there is a pine-cone. The plaque is broken at the bottom.

D2. A marble plaque found March 19, 1937 in the Athenian Agora, in a well of the Roman period on north slopes of Areopagus. Now in Agora museum.
Dimensions: Height 26 cm., width 20 cm., thickness 6.7 cm.

Bibliography: *AJA*, XLI, 1937, p. 183, fig. 10; Lane, I, p. 8, note 10.

The plaque, left somewhat unfinished, portrays an apparently female draped bust, with moon-crescent at neck, but without Phrygian cap.

DUBIA

Serdica: Sofia, Bulgaria

D3. Two fragments of a marble plaque, found the end of August, 1906, at "47 Wesletzstrasse" in Sofia; now in the Sofia Museum.

Dimensions: Height 52 cm., original width figured to be 70 cm., preserved width?; thickness 7 cm., height of letters, Latin inscription 3-4 cm., Greek inscription 1-2 cm.

>Bibliography: *B. Filow, *Sbornik za narodni umotvorenia*, XXII, 1907, 1ff.; Filow, *Klio*, IX, 1909, p. 253ff.; O. Walter, *AM*, XXXV, 1910, pp. 139ff.; Lane, I, p. 12, note 22.

The stone bears an inscription on one side in Greek, the letters pointing to the period 250-300 A.D. The inscription follows:

['Αγαθῇ Τύ]χῃ

[Οὐαλ]ερία
μήτηρ δενδροφόρ(ων)
Παρ[ι]άς
[Π]α[ύ]λου Ὠβείου
[γ]υ[ν]ή
two lines illegible
Κυρία γ[υν]ή
Μιθραδάτου
Οὐέρουλα
Χρυσάνθη
Ἡράκλια
Αὐρηλία
Νοντιανή

one
column
missing
completely

[····]α
[γυν]ὴ Δρά-
[κ]οντος
Ζωίλου

β'
[····]δώρα Λούππου
[····]α Ἰουλιανοῦ
[····]η μεμυίασα στολίδος
[ἱε]ροῦ δούμου
[ταῖ]ς μυστρίαις

On the other side there is an earlier inscription in Latin, apparently of the reign of Hadrian. It is variously restored, and I will first give Filow's restoration, then that of Walter:

P[ro salute]
Imp. C[aes. Traiani]
H[adriani Aug.]
Str[.........]
N[...sodalicium]
verna[culorum aedem]
de s[ua pecunia]
Matri Deum [Magnae]
fec[it cur(ante) ..Ty-]
ranno per M. Iu[lium? Satur?-]
ninum sacer[dotem].

For Tyrannus as a proper name Filow cites *CIL*, III, 10329. Cf. also our no. 65.

Pro [salute]
imp. C[aes. Traiani]
H[adriani Aug.]
Str[atonicus? Caes(aris) *or* Aug(usti)]
n(ostri) [ser(vus)]
Verna [arcuarius?]
de s[ua pecunia]
Matri Deum [Mag(nae) Id(aeae)]
fec(it) [et Atti Menoty-]
ranno per M. Iu[lium *or* -nium Satur- *or* Anto-]
ninum sace[rdotem.]

Both authors agree that the words after *fecit* seem to have been added by a later and more careless hand.

If Walter's restoration is to be accepted, it must be remembered that the Hadrianic date puts it much earlier than the Attis-Menotyrannus inscriptions from Italy on the basis of which it is restored. Altogether, however, it gives the impression of a better reasoned and more satisfactory restoration than Filow's.

Philippi (area of Kavala, Greece)

D4. A rock-cut relief discovered before 1865 by L. Heuzey. Dimensions unavailable.

Bibliography: L. Heuzey, *RA*, 1865, I, p. 456-458; *CIL*, III, 636; L. Heuzey and H. Daumet, *Mission Archéologique de Macédoine*, Paris, 1876, p. 83-85, no. 4 and Pl. IV, no. 1; Drexler, *op. cit.*, col. 2730; *Perdrizet, *Cultes et Mythes du Pangée*, p. 86, note 3; Keune, Pauly-Wissowa, *Real-Encyclopädie*, Suppl. III, 1918 s.v. Felsendenkmäler, col. 488, no. 50; C. Picard, *RHR*, LXXXVI, 1922, pp. 188-194; P. Collart, *Philippes, Ville de Macédoine*, Paris 1937, p. 438 and Pl. 77, no. 1; Lane, I, p. 11, note 17.

The relief shows a figure standing, with dress reaching to the knees, staff in left hand, object (broken off) in outstretched right hand, crescent at neck, and tall headdress (mutilated face). As far as the image itself is concerned, it would pass for a representation of Men. Doubt is cast on the identification, however, by the neighbouring inscription, itself with crescent and pair of eyes (*CIL*, III, 636; Collart, p. 441 and Pl. 77, no. 2), which, although hard to read, would seem to be a dedication to Diana.

Area of ancient *Dyrrachium* or *Epidamnus*: Kavaia, Albania

D5. Small portable altar discovered in 1861 or 1862 at Kavaia, near Durazzo, Albania (ancient Dyrrhachium or Epidamnus). Letter fails to bring information as to present whereabouts, etc.
Dimensions unknown.

Bibliography: *CIL*, III, 603; Heuzey and Daumet, *op. cit.*, p. 390; N. Gostar, *Dacia*, NS, IV, 1960, p. 522, note 15; Lane, II, p. 44, note 6.

The stone bears the inscription: (*CIL*'s version)

I O R - MENI - AUG
SIR/F/ /V - ARETE
V - S - L - M

Gostar, *loc. cit.*, would like to amend the first line into IOM - MENI - AUG and understand the inscription as a dedication to Jupiter Optimus Maximus, Men, and the Emperor, all being identified with each other. In view of the doubts expressed about other identifications of Men with the emperor Lane, II, pp. 42-44, I would also hesitate before accepting this one.

Carthago: near Tunis, Tunisia

D6. Fragment of a terra-cotta statue found in 1899 in Gauckler's excavations on the site of Carthage. Now in the Musée du Bardo.
Dimensions: Height 45 cm.

> Bibliography: P. Gauckler, *CRAI*, 4th Ser. XXVII, 1899, p. 159; *Bull. Arch du Comité*, 1899, p. CLXI; G. Perrot, *Revue de l'art ancien et moderne*, VI, 1899, p. 7-9 (with illustration); École Fr. de Rome, *Mélanges d'archeologie et d'Histoire*, 1900, p. 117; *S. Gsell, *Musée de Tebesa*, Paris, 1902, p. 75; H. Collignon, *RA*, 1903, I, p. 11, note 2; W. Deonna, *RA*, 1906, II, p. 408; *Les Statues de Terre Cuite dans l'Antiquité*, Paris, 1908, p. 198ff.; *Musée Alaoui*, Catalogue Supplement (1910), p. 152, nos. 187-8.

The fragment illustrated by Perrot (I can gather no information as to the other fragment) shows a leg with soft shoe and long, tight-fitting pants, placed on the head of a bull. (Other items reported by the catalogue of the Musée Alaoui as representing Men are definitely to be rejected.)

Antiocheia Pisidiae: Yalvaç, Turkey

D7. Marble relief broken on all sides, but particularly on the top and left. Found by Ramsay in 1912 excavations at Antioch in Pisidia. Now in İstanbul Museum.
Dimensions: Height 15.5 cm., width 19 cm., thickness 7 cm.

D 7

Bibliography: G. Mendel, *Catalogue*, III, p. 594, no. 1383; Lane, I, p. 35, note 130.

The relief shows a figure on horseback in military dress, holding a sword or short spear in his right hand, his left hand (broken) raised as if to hold something else. To the right, a naked groom, whose head is missing, holds the horse by the bridle. The head and crescent moon (if there was one) of the main figure are gone, and while it is not certain that Men is intended to be portrayed, the representation is not inconsistent with known armed representations of the god.

Korykos: near Kız Kale, Cilicia, Turkey

D8. Inscription next to door of grave-chamber, cut in rock. Dimensions: Letters of last word, 3.5 cm.

Bibliography: J. Keil and A. Wilhelm, *MAMA*, III, (1931), pp. 122 and 181-2.

According to the editors, the main inscription is Christian sepulchral, and reads:

Σωματοθήκη Λε-
οντίου καπίλου
'Αναστα[σ]ί[ου]

Underneath there is an altar in relief, dating, according to the editors, from an earlier use, with the inscription on the shaft: Μηνί.

Given the absence of other testimonia of Men-worship from this area, and the lack of an illustration, I would suspect rather the name (in the genitive): Μηνᾶ.

"Midas City", Yazılıkaya, S. of Seyitgazi
and S.E. of Kırka, Turkey

D9. Fragmentary marble statuette, found between 1937 and 1939 by the French excavators. Now in Istanbul Museum.
Dimensions: Height ca. 12.2 cm.

Bibliography: C. H. E. Haspels, *Institut Français d'Archéologie, Istan-*

bul, Phrygie, Exploration Archéologique, III, La Cité de Midas, Céramique et trouvailles diverses, (1951), p. 116, and Pl. 45, c 1; L. Robert, *Hellenica*, X, 1955, p. 16.

The statuette represented a barbarian horseman with long pants, riding right. There are preserved only the horse's torso and the rider's leg and hip, with part of his chiton. Designed to be seen from one side only, the back being roughly finished. The rider's leg, below the horse, is applied against a pilaster serving to support the statuette. L. Robert is responsible for the tentative identification as Men, by comparison with our number 159.

Cremna: Gürme, Turkey

D10. A portion of a gable from a ruined building. Known since 1885.

Dimensions: Height 56 cm., original width 2.64 m., (24 cm. at left missing).

Bibliography: Drexler, *op. cit.*, col. 2723; K. Lanckoronski-Brzezie, *Städte Pamphyliens und Pisidiens*, Vienna 1890-92, II, p. 171.

According to Lanckoronski, there is in the middle, heavily damaged, so that hardly anything more than the outline is recognizable, a human figure with pointed cap, frontally represented. There are preserved only the stumps of the arms. From its shoulders the points of a crescent moon protrude. Thus definitely the god Men, much worshipped in these areas.

Until the monument can be reexamined and photographed, I reserve judgment.

ADDENDA

Shortly after I submitted the manuscript for this volume to the publisher, two important new articles bearing on the cult of Men became available to me. The first is by Peter Herrmann and Kemal Ziya Polatkan, *Das Testament des Epikrates und andere neue Inschriften aus dem Museum von Manisa* in *Österreichische Akademie der Wissenschaften, Phil.-Hist. Klasse, Sitzungsberichte*, CCLXV, i, 1969. The other is by Barbara Levick, *Dedications to Men Askaenos* in *Anatolian Studies*, XX, 1970, pp. 37-50. The latter article I knew to be in preparation, and hoped that it would appear before my book, so that I could take advantage of Miss Levick's edition of the Men material from the Konya Museum. Both articles contain a number of new documents, as well as additional information on items included in the body of this book.

A 1. Stone of unknown description, copied by Alfred Philippson in Menye in 1901.

Dimensions unknown.

> Bibliography: P. Herrmann and K. Z. Polatkan, *op. cit.*, p. 39.

The stone bears the following inscription:

> Μέγας Μὶς 'Αρτεμιδώρου "Αξ-
> [ι]ττα κατέχων καὶ ἡ δύνα-
> [μ]ις αὐτοῦ.

Rest of inscription lost.

In connection with this inscription, the authors suggest that the place name "Αζιττα which occurs in our numbers 43 and 44 should actually be read "Αξιττα. I think they are right.

A 2. A stele of white marble, broken at bottom. Brought at unknown time from Kula to Museum of Manisa.

Dimensions: Height 54.5 cm.; width 42 cm.; thickness 5 cm.; height of letters 2 cm.; interlineation 1 cm.

> Bibliography: P. Herrmann and K. Z. Polatkan, *op. cit.*, p. 57, no. 13, and fig. 17.

The stone bears a sunken relief-field off-center to the right over the writing. It shows, left, a boy, draped, and, right, a woman, draped, with her right hand raised. To the left of the relief there is the following inscription:

Μηνὶ Ἀξιοττηνῷ ἐξ
Ἀπολλωνίου Γ(άϊος) Ἰ(ούλιος) Ἀνεί-
κητος μετὰ καὶ Ἰ(ουλίας) Τύ-
χης τῆς συνβίου ὑπὲρ
[.....]ήθου τοῦ υἱοῦ εὐ-
[χὴν ἀνέθη]καν τοὺς
....

A 3. A block of white marble, broken in two pieces and injured on the right side. Brought from Hamidiye (in the area of Kula) to the Museum of Manisa in 1962.

Dimensions: Height 28 cm.; width 62 cm.; thickness 38 cm.; height of letters 1.3 cm.; interlineation 0.6 cm.

Bibliography: P. Herrmann and K. Z. Polatkan, *op. cit.*, p. 55, no. 12·

The stone bears the following inscription:

Τατιαν Ἑρμοκράτους Βάσσαν ἱέρειαν Μηνὸ[ς Ἀξι-]
οττηνοῦ οἱ καταλουστικοὶ ἐτείμησαν διά τε τὴν ἰς [τοὺς]
θεοὺς εὐσέβειαν καὶ θρησκείαν καὶ τὴν πρὸς π[άντας]
ἀνθρώπους φιλοκἀγαθίαν, ἀναστραφεῖσαν ἐπὶ τῷ θε-
ῷ ἀφιλοκέρδως παντὶ τῷ βίῳ διὰ γένους. Ἀνεστάθη
δὲ ἔτους σμδ', μη(νὸς) Γορπιαίου βι', ἐπιμελησαμένου
Φιλοξένου β' γραμματέως, ζώσης ποιήσαν-
τες τὴν τειμὴν οἱ καταλουστικοὶ
ἐκ τῶν ἰδίων.   159-60 A.D.

Herrmann and Polatkan also report that our number 66 is now in the Manisa Museum (*op. cit.*, p. 57).

They also publish our no. 85 (*op. cit.*, p. 54, no. 11 and fig. 13) with the information that it is from Menye and with the following dimensions: height 88 cm.; width 29 cm.; thickness 27 cm.; letters 1.7 cm.; interlineation 0.7 cm.

In lines 5-7 they read

> 'Αρτέμων ΤΟ
> ΠΙΑΡΙΣ κατ' ἐπ[ι-]
> (τα)γὴν·········

and are undecided whether τὸ πίαρις = τὸν βωμόν or is a proper name. My reading, confirmed by the photograph, is not πι, but rather πη in ligature.

Miss Levick's article contributes two new monuments, one of them to be classed under 'dubia'.

A 4. The upper part of a pedimental stele, broken at left, presumably found at same time and same place as numbers 260-294. In 1955 in Konya Museum, but not to be seen there in 1969.

Dimensions: 21.5 by 28 cm.; letters irregular.

Bibliography: B. Levick, *AS*, XX, 1970, p. 46, no. 24.

"The stele is decorated with a crescent inside a wreath, surmounted by two crescents (surviving from the original four), and there is a crescent within the pediment."

The stone bears the following inscription, the first line being between the pediment and the main panel, the second in the main panel, interrupted by the wreath, and the last two within the wreath, above the crescent:

> ριχ καὶ 'Αττικιανός ⚘
> [τεκμορ]εύσαντες
> [μετὰ ἀ]δελφῆς κ[αὶ]
> [θ]ρεπτ[···]

A D 1. A marble fragment of irregular shape, presumably discovered at Yalvaç at the same time as nos. 260-294. Seen by Barbara Levick in 1955 in the Konya Museum.

Dimensions: 28 by 21.5 cm.; letters 5 cm. in first line, 3.8 in second.

Bibliography: B. Levick, *AS*, XX, 1970, p. 37, no. 1; and Pl. Ia, no. 2.

The fragment seems to show the forelegs of a bull, standing right before an altar. There also seems to be a ritual implement of some sort between the bull's legs.

166   CATALOGUE

Under the relief, the following inscription can be restored:

[L. Flav]oṇiu[s]
[Pau]llin̠[us]

The piece can probably be ascribed to Men on the basis of parallels. Cf. nos. 177, 280, and 288.

Miss Levick also contributes much to our knowledge of other inscriptions in the Konya Museum.[1] In most cases, my dimensions differ slightly from hers, however. I give below a concordance of numbers, with any major differences between our readings:
  our 162 = Levick, appendix no. 4, p. 49, and Pl. IIa, no. 3.
  our 250 = Levick, appendix no. 6, p. 49, and Pl. Va.
  our 260 = illustrated by Levick, Pl. Vb.
  our 262 = illustrated by Levick, Pl. IVb, no. 2.
  our 263 = Levick, appendix no. 4, p. 49, and Pl. IIIb, no. 1.
Miss Levick's conjectural restorations now differ in a few details from those she supplied me earlier by letter.
  our 264 = Levick, Pl. IIa, no. 2 and p. 42.
  our 265 = Levick, appendix no. 3, p. 49 and Pl. IIb, no. 1.
Miss Levick suggests the following restoration of the first two lines:

[Δέ]χμο[ς]
[Λ]ουκί[λιος]

  our 268 = Levick, appendix no. 1.
According to Levick's information, this piece is not from Yalvaç, but from İsparta. This does not agree with the information now to be gathered from the Konya Museum.
  our 270 = Levick, p. 47, no. 26, and Pl. Vc, no. 2.
  our 271 = Levick, p. 49, appendix no. 2, and Pl. IVa, no. 2.
  our 272 = Levick, p. 43, no. 12.
  our 273 = Levick, p. 38, no. 3.
Miss Levick's restoration is as follows:

Γ. Νεικάνορο[ς Νει-]
κάνωρ Ἀλέξαν[δρος]
σὺν τοῖς ἰδίοις [θρε-]

[1] The items which Miss Levick publishes, *op. cit.*, p. 38, no. 2 and p. 45, no. 20, have no internal evidence to connect them with the cult of Men.

πτοῖς τεχμορε[ύσας Μην-]
ὶ Ἀσκαηνῷ [εὐχήν.]

our 274 = Levick, p. 47, no. 25.
Miss Levick reads the beginning of the inscription as follows:

....
μον[ος μετὰ Ἔρω-]
τος etc.

our 275 = Levick, p. 42, no. 11 and Pl. IVa, no. 3.
Miss Levick reads the first two lines as follows:

[·····]τιος Ἀνίκ-
[ιος] τ[ὸ] τρίτον

our 276 = Levick, pp. 44, no. 17.
Miss Levick suggests the name

[Σύμ]φορος

in the next to last line.

our 277 = Levick, p. 46, no. 23.
In the last line, Levick reads

[···τέ]κνων where we read μνόη.

our 278 = Levick, p. 41, no. 9.
our 279 = Levick, p. 48, no. 27 and Pl. Vc, no. 3.
Levick hesitantly reads Οὐσέλλιος instead of Οὐίσεννος.
our 280 = Levick, p. 45, no. 21.
our 281 = Levick, p. 46, no. 22.
Miss Levick experienced difficulty in reading this inscription, but at the time of my visit I found it legible.

our 282 = Levick, p. 44, no. 18 and Pl. IVb, no. 3.
Levick reads:

[·····]Λουκ[ια]ν   ός
β[·····]ν [··Ζ]ωτικῷ σύν.

our 283 = Levick, p. 43, no. 13.
For the beginning of this inscription, Miss Levick reads:

[··]ΛΒΡ[····]Ι κοπτο-
πώλης

She interprets κοπτοπώλης as meaning "confectioner", or "seller of pastries."

our 284 = Levick, p. 42, no. 10, and Pl. IVa, no. 1.
our 285 = Levick, p. 44, no. 16, and Pl. IVb, no. 1.
For the last two lines, Miss Levick reads:

[···]εμιοι Συμφ[····]
[Σ]όφιμος Μακε[δών].

For the first word of the last line I prefer [T]ρόφιμος, and my copy shows distinct traces of the ρ.

our 286 = Levick, p. 43, no. 15.
For the first two lines, Miss Levick reads:

Αὐτρόνιος
Μάρκε[λλ]ος

our 287 = Levick, p. 40, no. 6, and Pl. IIIa, no. 2.
For the first line, Miss Levick reads:

[····]ουιος ΤΑΡΣ[····]

our 288 = Levick, p. 40, no. 5, and Pl. IIIa, no. 1.
For the first two lines, Miss Levick reads:

[··Μο]υνήτιος Πωλί-
[ωνος] Αὐξάνων etc.

our 289 = Levick, p. 41, no. 7 and Pl. IIIb, no. 2.
our 290 = Levick, p. 39, no. 4 and Pl. IIb, no. 2.
our 291 = Levick, p. 41, no. 8 and Pl. Ia, no. 1.
For the first line, Levick reads:

Γ. Ἥουειος Μάρκος

our 292 = Levick, p. 43, no. 14.
our 293 = Levick, p. 45, no. 19, and Pl. IVb, no. 4.
our 294 = Levick, p. 48, no. 28 and Pl. Vc, no. 1.

Our number 53 has been mentioned by D. M. Pippidi, *Studii de Istorie a Religiior antice*, Bucharest, 1969, p. 230.

Our number 123 has now been published by C. Vermeule in

Burlington Magazine, CXIII, 1971, p. 71 and fig. 50. It is also illustrated *Boston Museum Bulletin*, LXVIII, 1970, p. 210, no. 18a.

Prof. Vermaseren has brought to my attention that a sarcophagus from Tomis, Rumania, bearing a representation of bucranium and balance remarkably similar to that on our number 142 was published by E. Coliu, *Istros*, I, 1934, pp. 81 f. The author wishes to connect the symbolism with Men-cult. (See also Silvio Ferri, *Arte Romana sul Danubio*, Milan, 1933, figs. 593-4).

G. Bordenache, *Dacia*, N.S.V, 1961, p. 209 and fig. 25, also wishes to connect with Men-cult a fragmentary relief from Histria, showing part of a scale. The present author does not find either attempt particularly conclusive.

J. and L. Robert, REG, LXXXIII, 1970, p. 443, no. 522 interpret the previously uninterpreted words of our no. 85 as a Hellenization of the Latin word *topiarius*, "landscape gardener".

TOPOGRAPHICAL INDEX

(Since the ancient names of many sites of Men-worship are unknown, I restrict myself to giving modern place-names. Even this is difficult, in view of the orthographical uncertainty of many Turkish place-names. I omit the dubious examples from the list.)

Greece
  Athens 1-7
  Delos 18-19
  Eretria 14
  Lindos 17
  Piraeus 8-9
  Rhodes 16
  Sounion 11-13
  Thasos 15
  Thorikos 10

Rumania
  Sarmizegetusa 20
  Turda 21

Italy
  Ostia 22
  Rome 23-27

Turkey
  Ağlasun 125
  Aivatlar 51
  Akören 126
  Alaşehir 82
  Andya 129
  Ankara 158-159
  Antalya 136-137
  Askeriye 124
  Assar Tepe 76
  Avdan 94-95
  Ayazviran 40-50
  Aziziye 128
  Belenli 104
  Bergama 30
  Burdur 121-123
  Büyük Beşkavak 111
  Çavdarlitepc-Sülümenli 117
  Çay 112-116

  Çoğu 105
  Darmara 75
  Dereköy 143
  Elmaçık 102
  Ennek 155
  Eskişehir 91
  Fasıllar 144
  Geyre 118-120
  Görnevit 56-57
  Gözören 107-109
  Güllük 133
  Gyölde 31-39
  Haçılar 106
  Hasanköy 100
  Hasarlar 89
  Hatunsaray 154
  Işıklı 101
  İncik 134
  İncikler 83
  İzmir 28
  Kaleköy 156
  Karaoba 72
  Kavacık 73
  Kavaklı 67-68
  Kırğıl 88
  Kırka 87
  Konya 145-153
  Köleköy 69-71
  Kula 58-66
  Kuyucak 92
  Kütahya 99
  Manisa 84-85
  Menye 52-55
  Ördekçi 131
  Pise 127
  Saracık 135
  Sart 77-81

Seyitgazi 96-98
Simav 90
Söpüren 93
Tefenni 103
Tekke 29

Topaklı 157
Uluborlu 130
Yağçı Oğlu 62
Yalvaç 160-295
Provenience unknown 138-142

(This index, like the museum index, does not include items listed among the addenda.)

MUSEUM INDEX

I list here all objects which are reliably reported to have been transported to museums, even though there may be no recent confirmation of the objects' continued presence there. I exclude items in the dubious category.

France
    Paris, Louvre   8

Germany
    Berlin, Staatliches Museum   7
    Bonn, Akademisches Kunstmuseum   140

Great Britain
    Aberdeen, University, Wilson
        Collection   259
    London, British Museum   102, 142
    Oxford, Ashmolean Museum   78

Greece
    Athens, Agora Excavations
        Museum   4
    Athens, National Museum
        (including Epigraphical Museum)   6, 9-10, 12-13, 28, 141
    Eretria, Archaiologikon Mouseion   14

Italy
    Ostia, Museo Archeologico   22
    Rome (Vatican City), Museo
        Vaticano   26, 27

Netherlands
    Leiden, Rijksmuseum van Oudheden   35, 60, 137

Rumania
    Bucharest, National Antiquities
        Museum   21

Turkey
    Afyon Karahissar, Arkeoloji
        Müzesi   112-117
    Ankara, Arkeoloji Müzesi   158-159
    Antalya, Arkeoloji Müzesi   104, 121
    Burdur, Arkeoloji Müzesi   125
    İstanbul, Arkeoloji Müzesi   84, 99, 175-177
    İzmir, Eski Arkeoloji Müzesi   87

Konya, Arkeoloji Müzesi	146, 149, 150, 152 (?), 153, 162, 249-250, 260-295
Manisa, Arkeoloji Müzesi	74, 85
Sart, Sardis Excavation Collection	39, 77, 80
Yalvaç, Arkeoloji Müzesi	253-255
United States of America	
Boston, Massachusetts, Museum of Fine Arts	63, 123
Cambridge, Massachusetts, Fogg Art Museum	138-139

It is a comment on the difficulty of dealing with this material that, of the 295 monuments catalogued, only 96 at the most, or approximately one-third, are properly housed in museums. The rest are all *in situ*, lost, in private hands, or unknown.

PLATES I - CV

PLATE I

(1)

PLATE II

(2)

PLATE III

(4)

PLATE IV

(6)

PLATE V

ΛΑΗΗΤΙΝΗΣ
ΕΡΩΤΙΩΝ
ΜΗΝΩΝ
ΕΠΙΜΕΡΕΑΣ
ΓΑΛΛΙΟΥ

(8)

PLATE VI

(9)

PLATE VII

(10)

PLATE VIII

PLATE IX

(12)

PLATE X

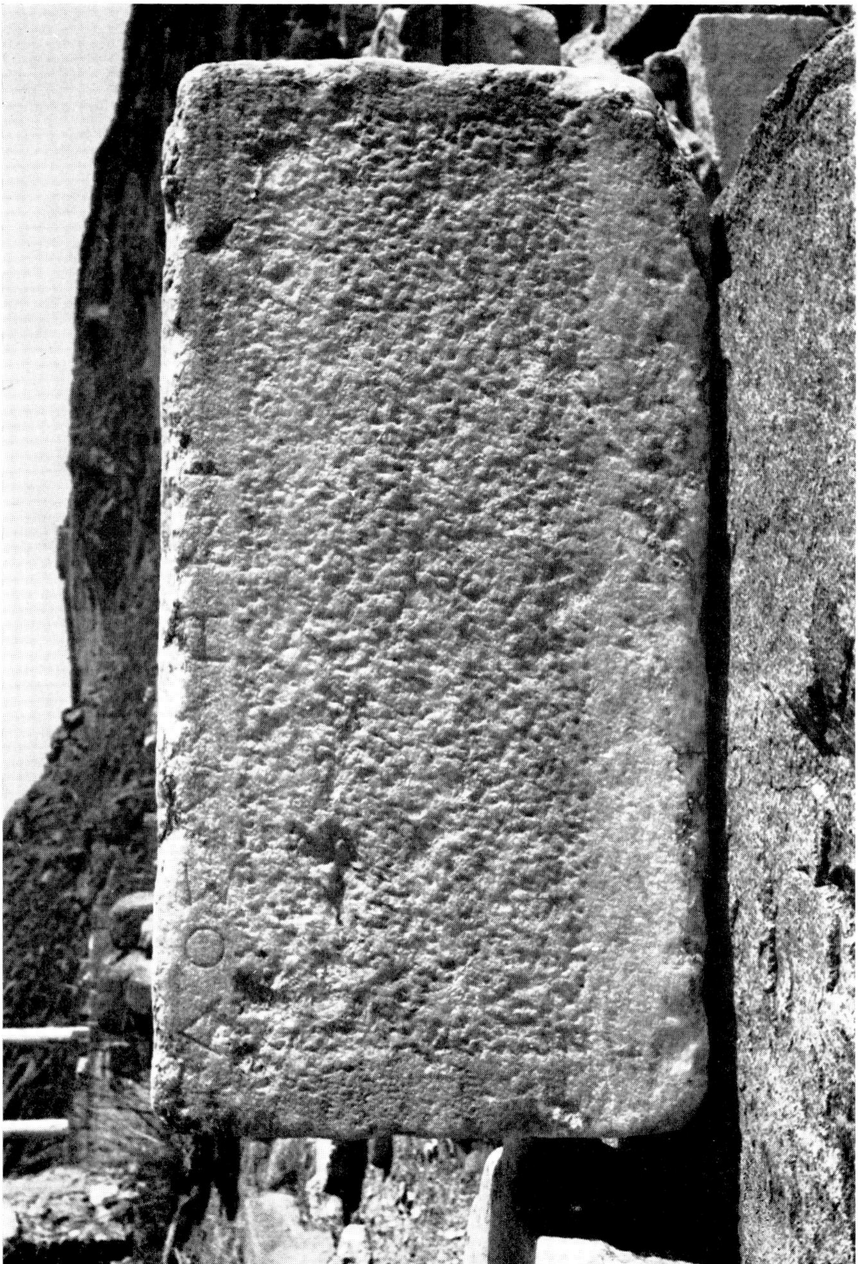

Photograph courtesy P. Bruneau

(18)

PLATE XII

PLATE XIII

(20)

(26)

PLATE XV

PLATE XVI

ΑΠΟΛΛΩΝΙΟΣ ΜΗΤΡΟΔΩΡΟΥ ΣΠΑΡΟ
Ο ΠΑΤΗΡ ΤΟΥ ΓΕΝΟΜΕΝΟΥ ΙΕΡΕΩΣ ΑΠ
ΛΩΝΙΟΥ ΤΟΥ ΑΠΟΛΛΩΝΙΟΥ ΣΠΑΡΟΥ
ΗΛΙΟΥ ΑΠΟΛΛΩΝΟΣ ΜΕΓΑΛΟΥ ΔΙ....ΟΥΛ
ΝΕΘΗΚΕΝ ΤΟΙΣ ΘΕΟΙΣ ΚΑΙ ΤΗ ΠΟΛΕΙ ΤΑ ΚΑΤΑΣΚΕ
ΑΣΘΕΝΤΑ ΥΠ ΑΥΤΟΥ ΛΑΒΩΝ ΚΑΤΑ ΨΗΦΙΣΜΑ ΤΗΝ
ΑΝΑΓΡΑΦΗΝ ΠΟΙΗΣΑΣ .....ΩΝ ΕΝ ΣΤΗΛΗ ΑΙ
ΕΣΤΙΝ ΑΥΤΟΣ Ο ΘΕΟΣ ΕΠ....ΜΑΤΟΣ ΜΑΡΜΑΡΙΝΟ
ΚΑΙ Η ΠΑΡΑΚΕΙΜΕΝΗ ΤΟΙΣ Θ..ΤΡΑΠΕΖΑ ΛΙΘΟΥ ΛΕΣΒΙ
ΟΥ ΕΧΟΥΣΑ ΠΟΔΑΣ Δ....ΤΟΥΣ ΓΡΥΠΑΣ ΚΑΙ ΠΡΟ ΑΥ
ΤΗΣ ΑΒΑΚΙΟΝ Μ....ΜΑΡ..ΟΝ ΠΡΟΣ ΤΗΝ ΧΡΗΣΙΝ ΤΩΝ
ΘΥΣΙΑΖΟΝΤΩΝ ΚΑΙ ΘΥΜΙΑΤΗΡΙΟΝ ΤΕΤΡΑΓΩΝΟΝ ΚΑ
ΤΕΣΚΕΥΑΣΜΕΝΟΝ ΠΕΤΡΑΣ ...ΗΙΑΣ ΕΧΟΝ ΠΕΡΙ ΠΥΡΟΝ
ΣΙΔΗΡΟΥ ΚΑΙ ΑΓΑΛΜΑ ΜΑΡΜΑΡΙΝΟΝ ΑΡΤΕΜΙΔΟΣ Ε
ΠΙ ΠΑΣ ΣΤΑΔΙ ΜΥΛΙΝΗ ΚΑΙ ΜΗΛΙΟΣ ΑΓΑΛΜΑ ΕΠΙ ΒΑΣΕ
ΜΑΡΜΑΡΙΝΗ ΚΑΙ ΤΡΑΠΕΖΑ ΠΟ..Η ΛΗ ΤΕΤΡΑΓΩΝΟΣ
....ΡΟΜΟΣ ΜΑΡΜΑΡΙΝΟΣ ΕΛΩΝ ΑΕΤΟΝ ΕΝ ΕΑΥΤΩ
ΔΙΟΣ ΚΑΙ ΝΑΟΣ ΕΞΥΛΩΜΕΝΟΣ ΚΑΙ ΚΕΚΕΡΑΜΩΜΕ
ΝΟΣ ΚΑΙ ΓΕΘΥΡΩΜΕΝΟΣ ΚΑΙ ΚΕΚΛΕΙΔΩ....
ΕΝΟ ΚΑΘΕΙΔΡΥΝΤΑΙ ΑΓΑΛΜΑΤΑ ΠΛΟΥΤΩΝΟΣ ΚΗ
ΛΙΟΥ ΚΑΙ ΚΟΥΡΗΣ ....ΣΕΛΗΝΗ ΣΕΠΙ ΒΗΜΑΤΟΣ
ΕΜΠΕΨΙΕΣΜΕΝΑ ΕΧΟΝΤΑ ΚΑΤΑΙΑΣ ΤΗΝ ΣΥΛΙ
ΝΟΝ ΝΑΟΕΙΔΕΣ ΚΑΙ ΤΑ ΣΤΟΝ ΛΙΝΟ...ΝΚΑΙ ΠΑΡ ΕΚΑΤΕ
ΡΑ ΤΟΝ ΕΙΣΟΔΩΝ ΒΩΜΟΣ ΣΦΩΡΑΙΚΟΣ ΚΑΙ ΚΛΕΙΝ
Η ΕΧΡΥΣΩΜΕΝΗ ΗΛΙΑ ΙΕΜΠΕ...ΑΣΜΕΝΗ ΗΝ ΠΡΟΣ
ΤΗΝ ΛΟΓΤΗΑΝ ΚΑΙ ΠΟΡΤΙ ΗΝ ΤΩΝ ΟΔΩΝ ΑΙ ΣΤΕΙ ΝΑ
ΕΠΙ ΠΕΔΑ ΚΑΙ ΕΠ ΑΥΤΟΙΣ ....ΤΟ ΑΝΚΑΤΩΡΟΔΟΜΗΜΕ
ΝΗΝ ΚΑΙ ΚΕΚΕΡΑΜΩΜΕΝΗΝ ΠΡΟΣ ΤΗΝ ΟΙΚΗΣΙΝ Τ Θ
ΙΕΡΟΔΟΥΛΟΥ ΤΑ ΠΟΝ ΘΕΟΝ ΘΕΡΑΠΕΥΟΝΤΩΝ ΚΑ
ΤΗΝ ΕΝΔΟΜΗΣΙΝ ΤΟΥ ΤΕΜΕΝΟΥΣ ΚΑΙ Ο ΘΕΜΕ ΛΙ
ΩΣ ΙΝ ΕΝ ΤΕΤΡΑΓΩΝΟ ΔΙΑΣΠΑΡΑΓΜΑΤΟΣ ΠΛ..
Η ΕΠΙ ΠΕΔΟΝ ΕΝΟΜΑΛΩ ΤΟ ΤΕΜΕΝΟΣ ΚΑΙ ΟΠΑ
ΤΟ ΙΟΘΕΩ ΠΑΡΑΚΕΙΜΕΝ ΑΤΟ ΥΡΟΣ.. ΜΟΥ ΧΑΡΙΝ
ΣΙΔΗΡΑ ΟΡΤΟ.

(28)

PLATE XVII

(35)

PLATE XVIII

(39)

PLATE XIX

(43)

Plate XX

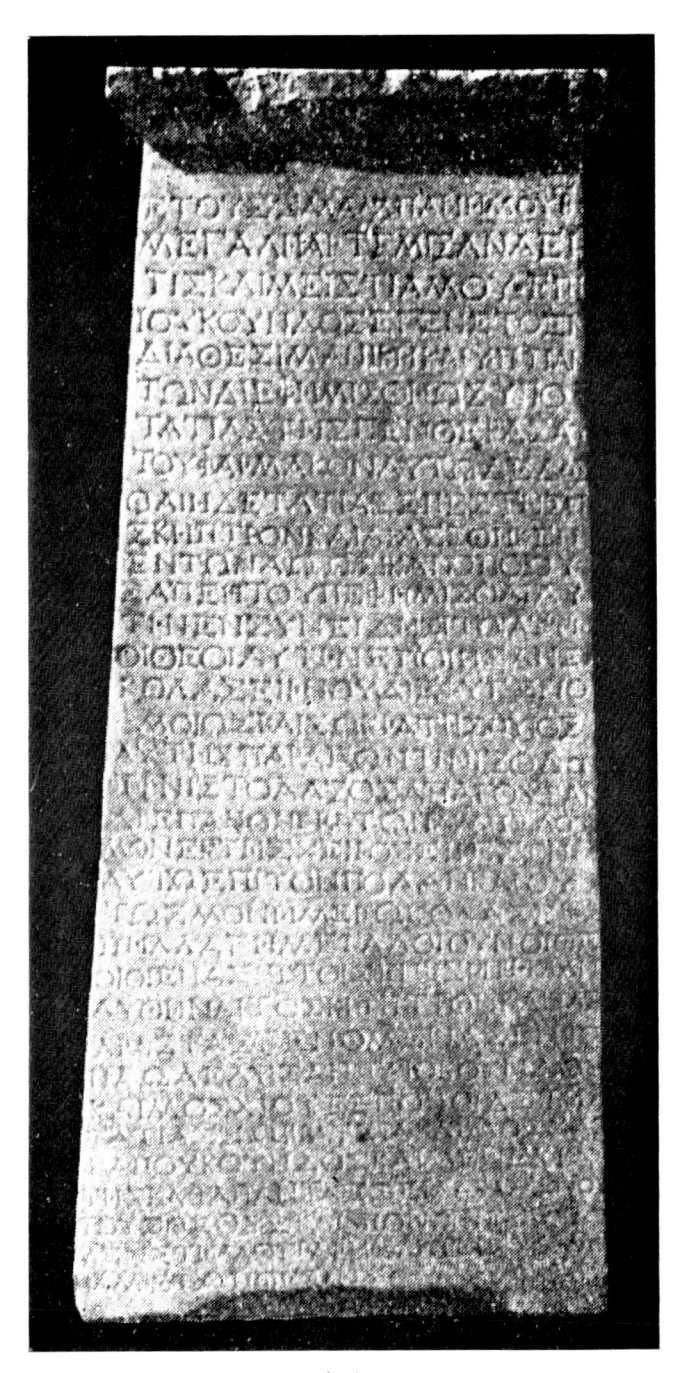

(44)

PLATE XXI

(47)

(48)

PLATE XXII

(50)

(49)

PLATE XXIII

(55)

(57)

PLATE XXIV

(60)

PLATE XXV

(63)

PLATE XXVI

(64)

PLATE XXVII

(65)   (66)

PLATE XXVIII

(67)

(68)

PLATE XXIX

PLATE XXX

(71)

(70)

PLATE XXXI

(74)

(73)

Plate XXXII

(78)

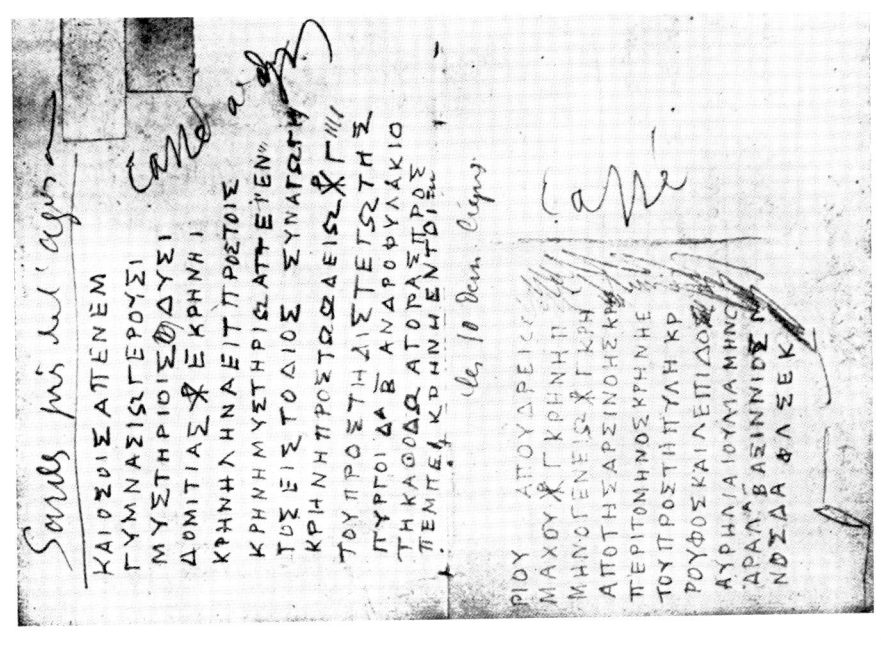

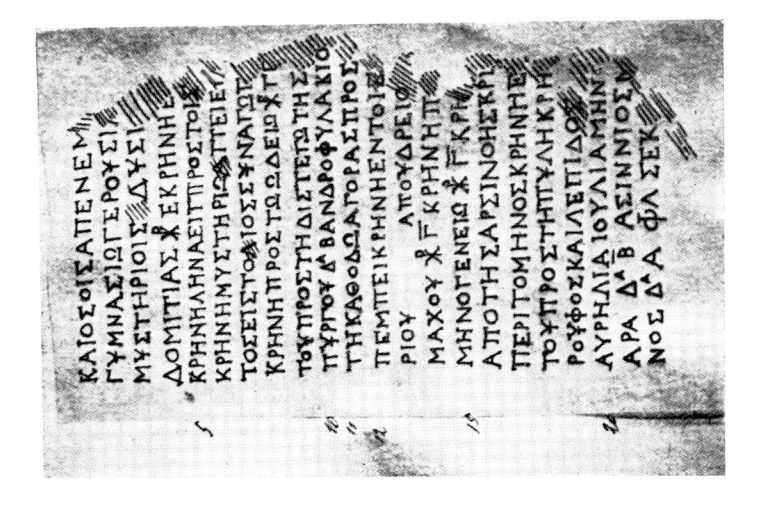

PLATE XXXIII

ΚΑΙ ΟΣΟΙΣ ΑΠΕΝΕΜ
ΓΥΜΝΑΣΙΩ ΓΕΡΟΥΣΙ
ΜΥΣΤΗΡΙΟΙΣ ⳨ ΔΥΣΙ
ΔΟΜΙΤΙΑΣ ⳨ Ε ΚΡΗΝΗ Ι
ΚΡΗΝΗ ΛΗΝΑΕΙ ΠΡΟΣ ΤΟΙΣ
ΚΡΗΝΗ ΜΥΣΤΗΡΙ⳨ ΑΠ ΕΤΕΝ"
ΤΟΣ ΕΙΣ ΤΟ ΔΙΟΣ ΣΥΝΑΓΩΓΗ
ΚΡΗΝΗ ΠΡΟΣ ΤΩ ΔΕ ΕΙΣ ⳨ Γ ΙΙΙΙ
ΤΟΥ ΠΡΟΣ ΤΗ ΔΙΣ ΤΕ ΤΣ ΤΗ Σ
ΠΥΡΓΟΙ Δ⁴ Β ΑΝΔΡΟΦΥΛΑΚΙΟ
ΤΗ ΚΑΘΟΔΩ ΑΓΟΡΑΣ ΠΡΟΣ
ΠΕΜΠΤΕΙ ΚΡΗΝΗ ΕΝ ΤΟΙΣ ⸗

ΡΙΟΥ ΑΠΟΥΔΡΕΙΣ
ΜΑΧΟΥ ⳨ Γ ΚΡΗΝΗ Ι
ΜΗΝΟΓΕΝΕΙΣ ⳨ Γ ΚΡΗ
ΑΠΟ ΤΗΣ ΑΡΣΙΝΟΗΣ ΚΡΗ
ΠΕΡΙ ΤΟΜ ΗΝΟΣ ΚΡΗΝΗΣ
ΤΟΥ ΠΡΟΣ ΤΗ ΠΥΛΗ ΚΡ
ΡΟΥΦΟΣ ΚΑΙ ΛΕΠΙΔΩ
ΑΥΡΗΛΙΑ ΙΟΥΛΙΑ ΜΗΝΟ
ΑΡΑ Δ⁴ Β ΑΣΙΝΝΙΟΣ ⸗
ΝΟΣ Δ⁴ Α ΦΛ ΣΕΚ

PLATE XXXIV

(80)

PLATE XXXV

(83)

PLATE XXXVI

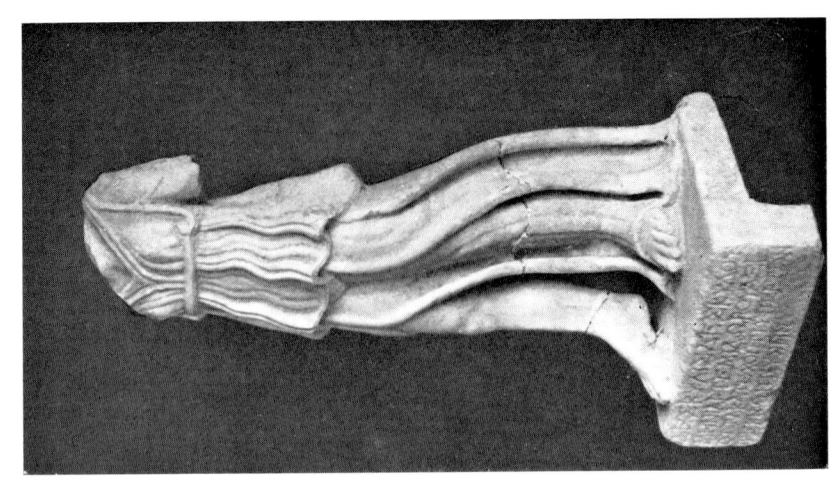

(86)

(85)

PLATE XXXVII

(87)

PLATE XXXVIII

(90)

PLATE XXXIX

(93)

(95) (94)

Plate XL

(96)

PLATE XLI

(97)

PLATE XLII

(98)

PLATE XLIII

(99)

Plate XLIV

(100)

PLATE XLV

(102)

PLATE XLVI

(104)

(105)

(107)

Plate XLVIII

(108)

PLATE XLIX

(112)

ΛΟΥΚΙΟΣ ΣΕΡ[
ΚΟΡΙΝΘΟΣ ΜΗ[
ΠΥΚΗΝΩ ΙΣ ΥΧΗΝ Α[
ΤΕ ΝΑΟΝ ΚΑΙ ΤΕ[
Ν ΔΟΝ ΕΚΤΩΝ ΙΔΙ[
ΕΠΩΙΗΣΕΝ ΕΤΟΥΣ[

(111)

PLATE L

(114)

(113)

PLATE LI

(115)

(116)

PLATE LII

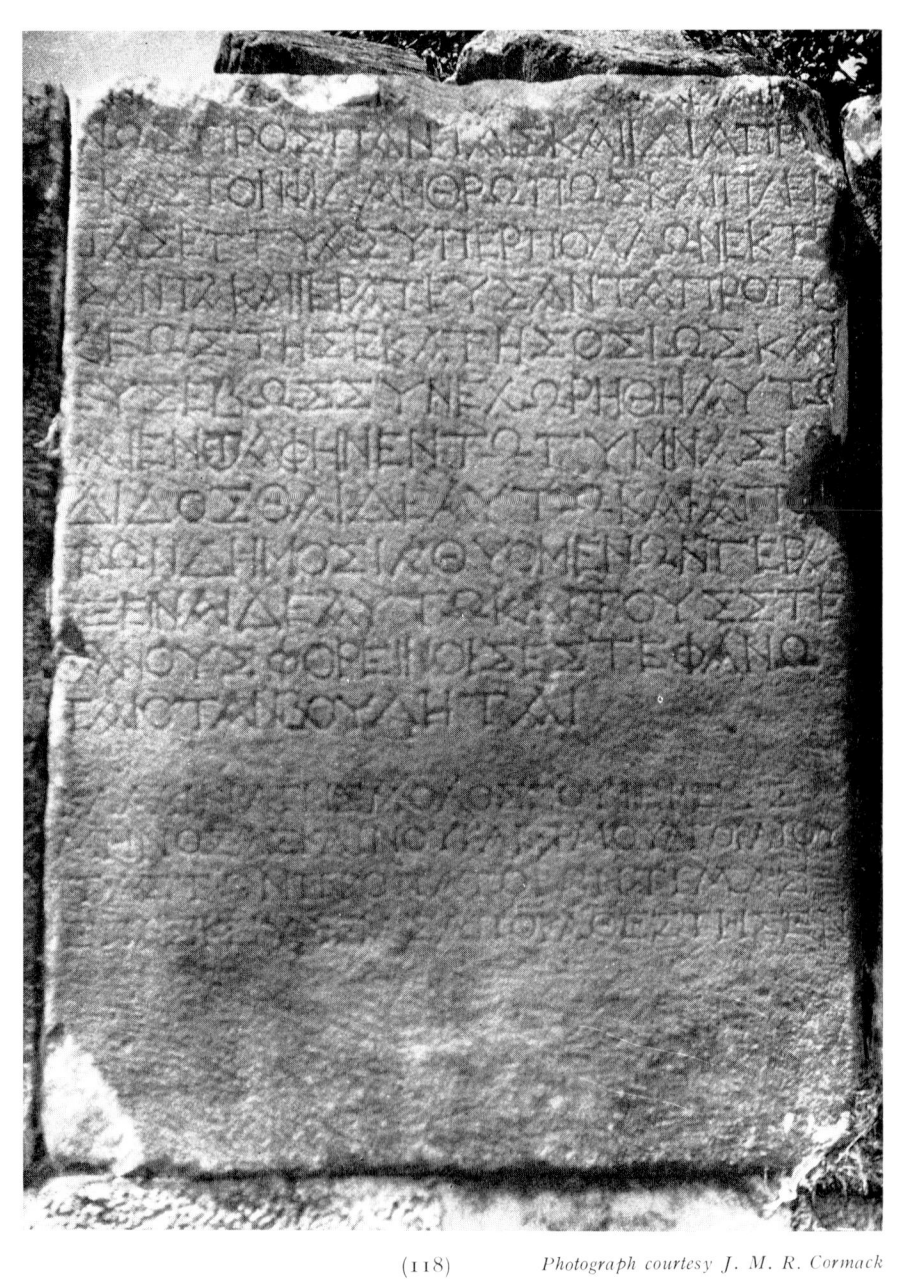

(118) Photograph courtesy J. M. R. Cormack

PLATE LIII

Photograph courtesy J. M. R. Cormack

PLATE LIV

(120)

PLATE LV

PLATE LVI

PLATE LVII

PLATE LVIII

(123)

PLATE LIX

(124)

Plate LX

PLATE LXI

(127)

(128)

ΙΟΥΛΙΑΝΔΟΥΙΕΡΕΑΕΞΙΕΡΕΩΝΜΗΝ

(131)

Plate LXII

(137)

PLATE LXIII

(138)

Plate LXIV

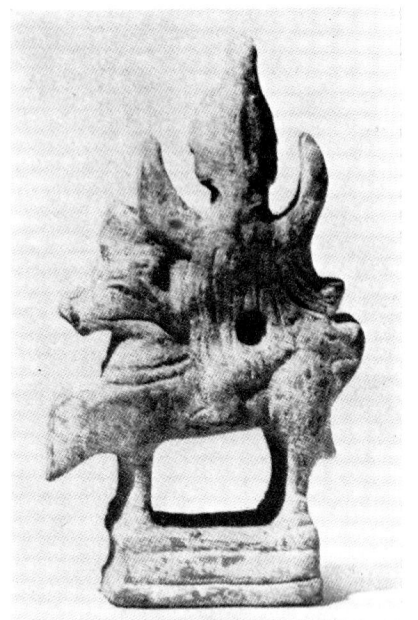

(139)

PLATE LXV

(140)

PLATE LXVI

(142)

(141)

PLATE LXVII

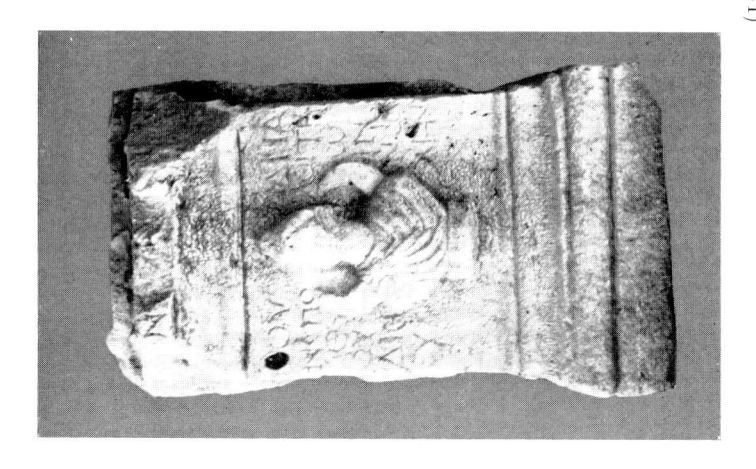

(153)

(149)

PLATE LXVIII

(158)

PLATE LXIX

(159)

PLATE LXX

PLATE LXXI

(164)

PLATE LXXII

ΕΠΙΑΓΩΝο
ΘΕΤοΥΛΙΑΒ
ΟΥΓΟΥΠΡ
ΟΥΒΛΙΒΙΛ
ΝΟΥΑΥΤΟΥ
ΡοΣΚΑΙΕΡ
ΩΣΛΙΑΒΙΟΥ
ΤοΥΠΥΓΙΟΥ
ΘΕοΥΜΗΝΟΣ
ΚΑΙΘΕΛΣΔΗ
ΜΗΤΡΟΣΛ
ΕΛΩΤΙΟΝ

(165)

PLATE LXXIII

(166) (167)

PLATE LXXIV

(169)

PLATE LXXV

(170)

(172)

(173)

PLATE LXXVIII

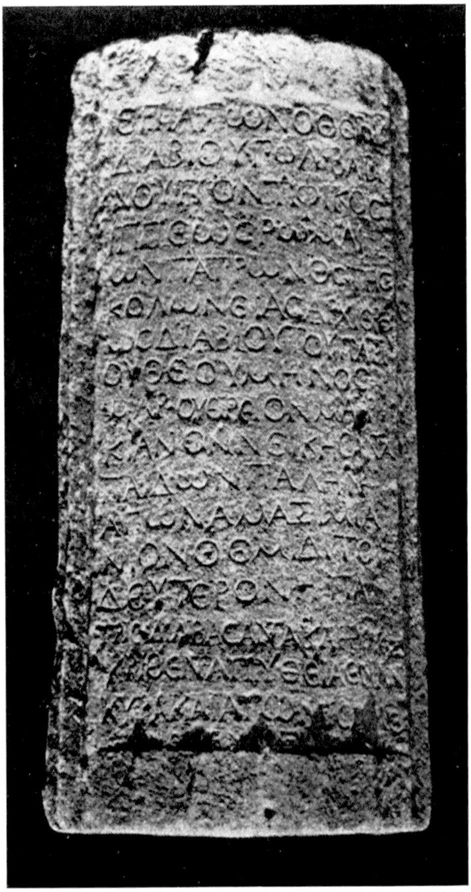

(174)

PLATE LXXIX

(176)

PLATE LXXX

(249)

(250)

PLATE LXXXI

(253) Photograph courtesy Yalvaç Arkeoloji Müzesi

(254)

Plate LXXXII

(255)

PLATE LXXXIII

(259)   *Photograph courtesy University of Aberdeen*

PLATE LXXXIV

(260)

PLATE LXXXV

(261)

PLATE LXXXVI

(262)

PLATE LXXXVII

(263)

Plate LXXXVIII

(264)

PLATE LXXXIX

(265)

PLATE XC

(268)

(267)

PLATE XCI

(269) (270)

PLATE XCII

(271)

(272)

(273)

(274)

PLATE XCIII

(275)

(277)

(276)

(278)

Plate XCIV

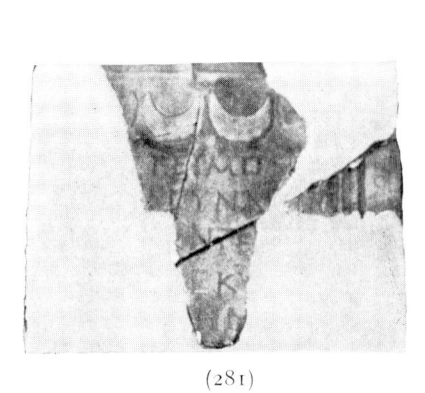

(279)

(280)

(281)

(282)

PLATE XCV

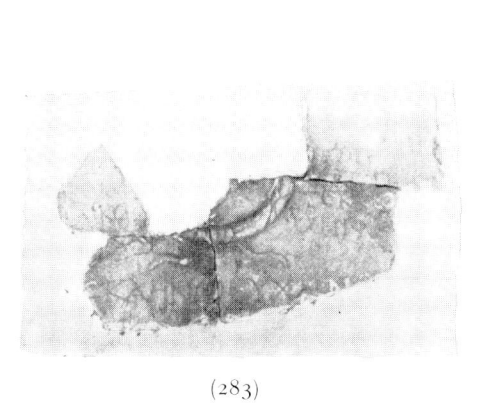

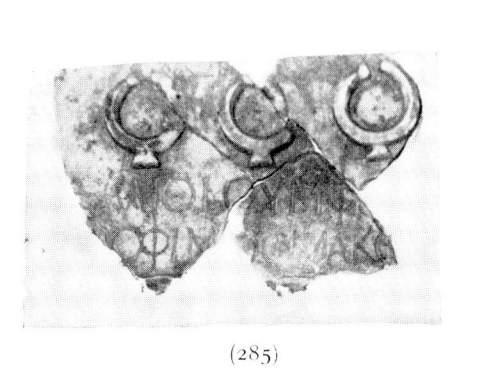

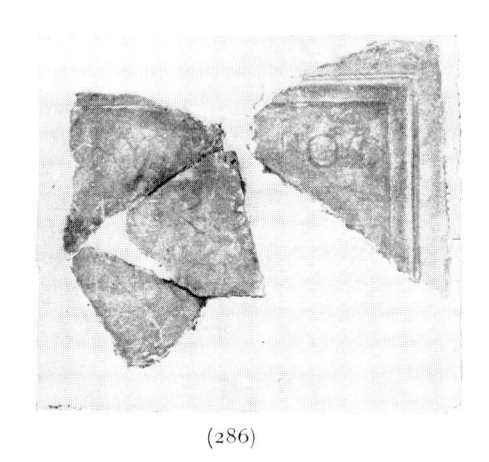

(283)

(284)

(285)

(286)

Plate XCVI

(287)

(288)

PLATE XCVII

(289)

(290)

PLATE XCVIII

(291)

(292)

(293)

(294)

PLATE XCIX

(D1)

Plate C

(D2)

PLATE CI

(D3)

PLATE CII

(D4)

PLATE CIII

(D6)

PLATE CIV

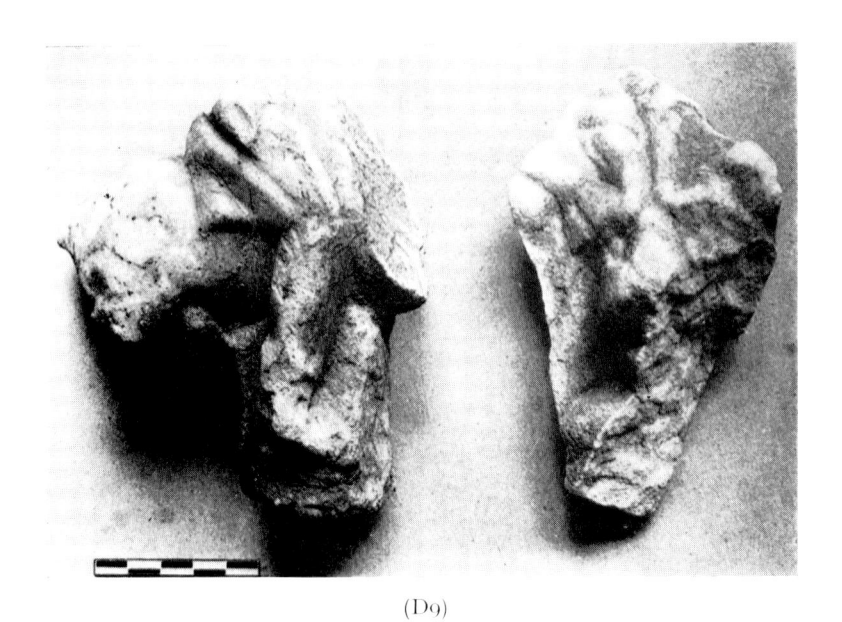

(D9)

PLATE CV

(A2)   (A1)

The Cult of THE GOD MEN
DISTRIBUTION-MAP
OF THE MONUMENTS
EUROPA-AFRICA
O DUBIOUS MONUMENTS
0 50 100 150 200 250 km
Potaissa
Sarmizegetusa
DACIA
PADUS
DANUVIUS
MŒSIA
ILLYRICUM
Serdica
THRACIA
TIBERIS
CORSICA
MARE
ADRIATICUM
Roma
Ostia
Dyrrhachium
EPIDAMNUS
Philippi
Thasus
ASIA
MINOR
ITALIA
MACEDONIA
SARDINIA
EPIRUS
MARE TYRRHENUM
Eretria
GRÆCIA
Athenæ
Thoricus
Piræus
Sunium
Delus
PELOPONNESUS
SICILIA
MARE IONIUM
Carthago
AFRICA
F.DERKSEN-JANSSENS 1971

The Cult of THE GOD MEN
DISTRIBUTION-MAP
OF THE MONUMENTS
ASIA MINOR
PERGAMUM : ANCIENT NAMES
Saracık : MODERN NAMES
(All I's have been written without dots)
O : DUBIOUS MONUMENTS
0 10 20 30 40 50 100 km
PONTUS EUXINUS
THRACIA
PROPONTIS
PAPHLAGONIA
SANGARIUS
HALYS
BITHYNIA
RHYNDACUS
MYSIA
GALATIA
ANCYRA
DORYLÆUM
ANDRONA? (Topaklı)
OUEDZA? (Söpüren)
AOUDA? (Avdan)
NACOLEIA
SEREA? (Kuyucak)
HASARLAR
COTTIÆUM
ALIANON KATOIKIA
PERGAMUM
"Midas City" (Yazılıkaya)
SYNAUS
Büyük Beşkavak
PHRYGIA
APPOLA? (Çoğu)
VETISSOS? (Yağçı Oğlu)
SAITTÆ
KAUALENON KATOIKIA
Çavdarlıtepe-Sülümenli
LYCAONIA
HERMUS
MOSTENE? (Assar Tepe)
SELMEA
ACMONEIA
JULIA (IPSUS?)
MAGNESIA AD SIPYLUM
MÆONIA
COLOE
ALIA? (Kırka)
SMYRNA
SARDIS
PHILADELPHIA
ANTIOCHEIA PISIDIÆ
LAODICEIA COMBUSTA
EUMENEIA
APOLLONIA
LYDIA
PLOURISTRA?
ANABOURA
Darmara
PISIDIA
MAGNESIA AD MEANDRUM
MEANDER
ICONIUM
SAVATRA
Askerıye
Fasıllar
APHRODISIAS
Burdur
SAGALASSUS
LYSTRA
CARIA
Azızıye
CREMNA
Dereköy
ORMELEIS
MACROPEDIUM
SIDIMARIA
OLBASA
PAMPHYLIA
ANDEDA
TERMESSUS
Incık
ATTALEIA
Saracık
RHODUS
RHODUS
LINDUS
LYCIA
MARE LYCIUM
F. DERKSEN-JANSSENS 1971
REGION OF COLOE - Kula
SAITTÆ
TARSI? (Köleköy)
Kalburcu
HERMUS
Kavaklı
Hamıdıye
Karaoba
Ayazvıran
Aıvatlar
Gyölde
MÆONIA
Kavacık
COLOE
Görnevit
0 2 4 6 8 10 km